Don't be afraid of your food storage...
just **Dutch it!**

No power? No problem!
Your guide to charcoal storage
and cooking

Don't be afraid of your food storage…just Dutch it!

Don't be afraid of your food storage…just Dutch it!

Created and compiled by: A&L Dixon Enterprises, formally Think'n Investments LLC

Authors: Archie and Linda Dixon
Cover and Art Work: Janine Madeiros
Editors: Leon and Charlene Papin and Danny Madeiros

ISBN 978-0-578-06197-9

Second Edition 2010

Printed in U.S.A. by:
Jostens
29625 Road 84
Visalia, CA 93291
559-651-3301

Preface

We would like to take a moment to explain how this book came to be. I believe we were inspired because one day it just hit me like a bolt of lightning: We need an instruction book on how to cook your basic food storage with charcoal and Dutch ovens!

We want to thank everyone who helped with this effort. It was a labor of love. We had lots of fun trying different recipes, and enjoyed eating all the food we cooked.

Please enjoy yourself. Have fun! All of us hope you will be better prepared and ready for whatever comes your way.

Thank you from:

Archie and Linda Dixon
Danny and Janine Medeiros
Leon and Charlene Papin

Table of Contents

We hope you enjoy this book. Let us know.
We would love to hear from you.
**Contact us at: 1-888-340-8947 or
justdutchit@yahoo.com**

Introduction

     Thank you for purchasing our book. We have had a lot of fun putting this book together and we hope you enjoy it. This book is more of a guide to the possibilities of what you can do with your food storage when the power is out. Have you ever considered how you would cook your food if you didn't have any electricity or gas? When you finish exploring this book, you will know how to solve this problem.

     We encourage you to try some of the recipes from each category, become familiar with how your Dutch oven works, and explore all the possibilities it brings. Don't wait until the power is off to try some of them in your Dutch oven. Learn how all this works *before* there is an emergency. Again, this is a guide to help you explore for yourself all that you can create with a little dehydrated food and a few canned items. We also wanted to get people excited about what they can cook with charcoal.

     You will find that we created recipes to reflect the type of foods most often stored. Our recipes will take you from good, to better, and then to best! **YUM!** Each recipe has a basic or "good" version. Then by adding one or two pantry items you can make that same recipe "better", add another item or two and you have the "best" version of the recipe. By adding just a few extra items to your basic food storage you will have a meal that tastes great and is easy to fix....because everyone likes great food, even in an emergency!!!

Enjoy!!!

Let's Get Started

Well now you've done it! You have all this wheat, milk, honey, beans, salt and a Dutch oven you were told to buy, so now what? You're not even sure you like wheat berries. What are wheat berries? TVP? What's that? Well, if you're like me, this was all kind of new. I wasn't sure I even liked any of this stuff... let alone how to fix it.

As I moved along in life, I was able to learn more and more about what this food was and how to prepare it properly. I learned how to make some items but wasn't sure on others...one thing was for sure, I didn't have any way to cook unless I was in the kitchen. Maybe the outside BBQ? How do you cook wheat on a BBQ anyway? I wasn't even sure we could always depend on having a BBQ available to our family. Then I started thinking about other methods of cooking. What if there was no electricity, natural gas, or propane?

We had inherited my father-in-laws 12" Dutch oven years ago. I then bought a 14" one as well. We got a few Dutch oven cook books and were on our way to learning how to use them. We cooked "Dutch" at family campouts and my wife was even asked to do a Dutch oven cooking class at church in the small rural community where we lived.

Then it all came together: Cook your food storage in your Dutch oven using charcoal! Why not? Charcoal is fairly cheap and easy to store. However, there was one problem. If we needed to depend on our basic food storage I couldn't find any information out there telling me how to cook with just the food that was stored in the closets and under the beds. We have come up with some basic recipes using just your stored foods and a few pantry items; nothing from the refrigerator or the freezer (if the electricity is out, all that food will either be spoiled or eaten up). Then, by adding just a few more items from your pantry, you can eat quite well. I hope you enjoy learning to cook with your Dutch ovens and charcoal. Don't just put this book in the closet next to all the wheat and powdered milk, use it to learn the basics before there is a real emergency.

As you move forward with your food storage you will need to make up your mind about what your goals are and what you would like to eat. There are many lists available to us that say you should have this or that. We have come to the following conclusion: Store food for you and your family that you like to eat! This needs to fit your budget and needs to be able to store well. We will help you discover what those foods are. We also have some ideas about charcoal storage and recipes that we think you will enjoy cooking and eating. You never know, it just might be fun!

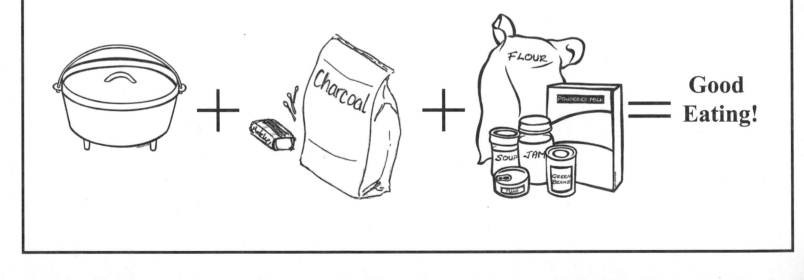

Buying a Camp Dutch Oven

You need to have a "camp" type Dutch oven. This is not the oven you find in your cooking magazines, but the kind you take camping and use for outdoor cooking with charcoal. It has a flat bottom and sits on three short legs. These legs allow you to move briquettes in and out from under the oven, regulating the oven temperature. The lid has a raised rim around the edge so coals will stay on top while cooking.

Now the big question…..what size do I need and how many ovens should I have? This is something you need to think about. If you will be getting just one, then the 12" oven is the best all-around oven to buy. I also like a 14" and a 10". With three ovens you can cook your meals very easily. This could change depending on how many people you are cooking for. Also you can take advantage of stack cooking. This maximizes your charcoal. Your top charcoal becomes the bottom for the one stacked on top. Notice how deep they are as well. You may want to have a deep oven for soups or cooking bread.

Be sure you get a good quality Dutch oven. I have found that different brands of ovens have lids that fit tighter than others. This is important for the efficiency of the oven. Also, you will find a tighter lid helps keep dirt out if you use it for deep pit cooking. Aluminum ovens are also available. I don't care for them; it seems un-natural for some reason. They work ok but seem to lose heat quickly. I just don't care for them.

Buying a Camp Dutch Oven cont.

If it's not made in the USA it might not be the best quality. We recommend the "Lodge" brand because of its superior craftsmanship. Dutch ovens, if taken care of, will last longer than you.

Care and Storage of Dutch Ovens

Preparing your New Dutch Oven

Wash your new Dutch oven (or the one you might have picked up at a yard sale) in hot soapy water and scrub off the protective wax or oil put on by the manufacturer (unless told otherwise per instructions with oven), then dry quickly. To do this use a stiff brush or green scrubbing pad. Dutch ovens are iron and will rust if not kept dry, even for a short time. This will be the only time you should need to use soap on your oven.

Now you need to "season" the oven. While still warm from washing, wipe the dry oven and lid all over with a lightly oiled paper towel or cotton cloth. Use regular vegetable oil. Don't pour oil directly into the oven. It's wasteful and may cause a build up. After oiling the Dutch oven, place it in your kitchen oven on the bottom rack at 350 degrees with lid ajar. Bake one hour. You may get strange smelling fumes so open a few windows. **(This process should be done before there is an emergency, ie. no power)**. If you can't use your kitchen oven and have a barbeque with a lid, you can do the same thing in it. Once the Dutch oven has cooled down, remove it, oil it, and bake it again. Leave it in the kitchen oven until warm, remove it, then oil it lightly one more time. Your Dutch oven is ready to use. You will notice it has turned a golden color, but after continued use it will have a black shine. This is what we want. If it does rust excessively, just repeat the above process.

Cleaning and Storage

After cooking in it, scrape it out with a spatula. After it has cooled slightly, put an inch or so of water in it (Do Not Put Cold Water In A Hot Dutch Oven, You Could Crack It!) and return to the coals to boil and steam out the stuck on food. After several minutes remove and when not too hot lightly scrub with a brush or cleaning pad. Rinse, dry, and lightly coat with oil. Before storing, fold up a small piece of foil or paper towel about 1/2" to 1" wide and 3" to 4" long and fold it over the edge of the oven. Put the lid on. This keeps the lid from sticking, especially if you are storing it for any length of time. Store it inside the garage or basement away from moisture.

Charcoal and How to Store It

Charcoal…what a wonderful fuel to store. It's safe, fairly cheap, and for the most part clean burning. We have found regular charcoal is best. You may want to stay away from the one match light starting types. These may cause an unsafe condition that could cause an explosion. Also if they get wet you will still have to start it the good old fashioned way.

We recommend having a charcoal chimney for starting your briquettes. We have found the Weber charcoal chimney to be way cool. It is large enough to start a large quantity of charcoal. A large chimney can be turned upside down and used as a charcoal stove. You also need lighter fluid or newspaper for starting the charcoal burning. And don't forget the matches!

The inverted chimney will boil 4 cups of water in about 25 minutes with about 25 briquettes. If you use this method, be sure the chimney is stable; you don't want it tipping over. Only use the large chimney this way. It works great for cooking eggs, pancakes, and fritters on the Dutch oven lid. Also, always cook in an area where you won't start a fire. Never cook on wood or plastic tables. Metal, brick, bare dirt or any non-flamable surface is the best area to use. **Do not use charcoal in an enclosed area**: inside house, garage, basement, etc. **It could be lethal!**

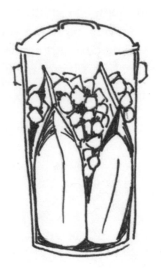

I store my charcoal in plastic garbage cans. I have them along the side of the house that nobody goes on. It's in the shade and for the most part out of the way. The people at Kingsford tell us their charcoal will store practically indefinitely so it may be around longer than us! Each meal takes 20 to 30 briquettes or about 1.5 pounds of charcoal. Now you might want to decide how many meals a day you will be cooking. If we are in an emergency condition you might want only two meals per day. With that thought in mind you only have to multiply the pounds of charcoal needed per meal, 1.5 lbs. x 2 meals, = 3 pounds x 365 days = 1,095 pounds for one year.

As I mentioned earlier, I have my charcoal in 32 gallon plastic garbage cans. One garbage can holds about 115 pounds of charcoal so that equals around 10 garbage cans full for one year. This will give you a good idea as to how much charcoal you need to store for your family. Also, we place two bags into the garbage can, then open the other bags and pour loose charcoal around the bags. This helps make the cans more stable.

See illustration.

How to turn off charcoal and save it

This is so simple to do. When I tell people about this they don't believe me but it's true. You just drop the hot briquettes into a pail of water. Bingo, it's out! Hey don't touch the water... it's HOT!!! After water has cooled, drain and let them dry out really well (usually a few days). After they are good and dry, just mix them in with your new ones and you have reused your charcoal.

The best part about knowing this is you don't have to be so worried about how much charcoal you use for each meal. It's better to have too much than not enough. You don't want your oven to cool down waiting for additional charcoal to be lit. Make plenty, cook, then just put them out when you are done and save what you don't use. As you cook more and more you'll get to know how much charcoal is needed to do your cooking. This is another good reason why you should practice cooking in your Dutch oven. Do it now!

Tools

Here is a list of the various tools you will need to have:

- Lid lifter and/or long handled pliers
- Heavy leather insulated gloves
- 16" or longer tongs
- Charcoal chimney starter (optional but almost a must have)
- Newspaper and/or lighter fluid
- Matches
- Long handled spoon
- Charcoal
- Vegetable oil and applying cloths or paper towels
- Bricks for lid cooking
- Cooking table (optional)
- Lid stand (optional)
- Temperature gun (optional)
- Aluminum foil (optional)

Tools cont.

You will need to have a tool to remove the lids. Several types are made that you can buy or you can use long handled pliers to do the same thing. My wife likes the pliers the best. She also uses them to lift cake pans and bread pans out of the ovens.

I have found the leather gloves you get at the welding shop work great. Be careful. When they get hot they stay hot.

Tongs are needed for moving the hot coals around. You will be moving coals around all the time so get these now. Regular long kitchen tongs are perfect.

A charcoal chimney starter is not a must, but your briquettes start a lot faster when you use one. If you need more coals in a hurry it is the best thing to use.

You need paper to put in the bottom of your chimney starter, so save a bunch of your old newspapers in a box to have when you need them. You can use charcoal lighter fluid, but your coals will cook too fast so just stick with the newspaper.

You will need MATCHES! You can also use flint and steel; just be sure you have a way to start a fire.

You will need a long handled spoon for stirring beans, soups, cereals, etc. You don't want to get burned. There is a lot of heat coming off those Dutch ovens.

Of course you need lots of charcoal. See the "Charcoal and How to Store It" section.

Oil and a way to apply it is a must. See the section on oil.

Tools cont.

Something that is very nice to have is a metal cooking table. I built one with angle iron and a piece of scrap metal. I salvaged the legs from an old folding table. It is a little heavy but works great. Also I have another cooking table made from a disk from a farm tractor. We welded 3 ½" unions on the bottom and made 3 pipe legs, then by welding I filled in the hole in the middle and there you go, one great cooking table. You can also purchase ready-made tables online. If you choose to cook on the ground, just buy plain 12" square concrete stepping stones. These make great cooking surfaces. We had a church Dutch oven dinner and had several dozen of the concrete squares on the patio. They worked great! You will need at least 3 concrete squares: one for the charcoal chimney, one for the Dutch oven, and one to set the Dutch oven lid on.

Having some type of stand to put the hot lid on is very helpful, as mentioned above. You don't want to set the hot lid in the dirt and then put it back on the Dutch oven after stirring your beans.   You could end up with dirt and bugs in your beans (of course you might like that) if you're not careful, so think of where you will set your lid during cooking.

Another tool I like is a temperature gun. This allows me to tell the temperature of the oven. It's amazing how the top part of the oven and the bottom can be so different in temperature. Also the gun really helps me when I'm making pancakes or frying on the lid. As you get more experience you will know how the placement of charcoal on the top and bottom works best for your oven. You don't need to have a temp gun, it's just kind of fun to play around with.

Aluminum foil is very handy to have. When I bake an Upside Down Cake or Cobbler directly in the Dutch oven, lining the oven with heavy duty foil makes a big difference when it comes to clean-up. Water for cleaning may be scarce, so this helps a lot.

Food Storage and Good, Better, Best

We hope this book will motivate you to expand your storage with the items you enjoy eating. Make meals more interesting. Have cocoa so you can make the kids brownies or cans of chicken for making chicken soup. When purchasing food items, be sure you consider any food allergies your family might have. As you add to your food storage it becomes something more than a bunch of boxes in the garage or basement. We hope you enjoy this experience as much as we did while we experimented cooking with foods that came only from our food storage or what was on the cupboard shelf.

How much should you store? There are plenty of lists and suggestions about how much of the basics to store, but what about the extras, like peanut butter or bouillon, tuna or baking powder? All you need to do is write down those pantry items you use all the time and figure out how often you might use them in an emergency situation. Figure out how much you use in a month and go from there. Take us for example; we use 4 to 6 cans of tuna each month, so for a year supply we would need about 50 cans. How much peanut butter do you use? Our Peanut Butter Cookie recipe is great and doesn't use any eggs, so I would add extra peanut butter if you thought you might make these often. Just take a few days, look through the book, and decide what recipes you like and come up with ideas of your own. Look at the meal plan in the next section and then you will have a better idea as to the types of meals you can make.

We recommend that you use your Dutch oven often; for cooking on your camping trips or in the back yard for Saturday night meals. This way you will be familiar with how your oven works. Then, if you start using it in an emergency along with your food storage, *bingo*, you are ready to go. The purpose for this book and the information we have put together will help turn your short and long term food storage into something you will enjoy. In our book we have three variations to most of the recipes. We show the basic "Good" version but also "Better" and "Best" versions. In the chart below we have listed the foods that are used to cook all the recipes in the book.

Food Storage and Good, Better, Best cont.

As you can see, by adding just a few more items, you can take the "Good" recipes all the way to "Best". The items are organized into categories. Water is used in preparing all recipes. Be sure you have plenty of water stored.

The following food items are needed to make all the "Good" recipe versions:

Whole wheat flour	Dried carrots	Vanilla	Sage	Tomato sauce/paste
Cracked wheat	Dried apple slices	Cornstarch	Canned/dried green	Canned tomatoes
Whole wheat berries	Instant potatoes	Beef bouillon	beans	Canned chicken
Rolled oats	Macaroni	Chicken bouillon	Canned/dried corn	Canned tuna
Salt	Spaghetti	Chili powder	Dried green bell	Canned beef
Oil	Dried potato slices	Ground cumin	pepper	Canned clams
Shortening	Dried shredded	Nutmeg	Dried celery	Soy sauce
Sugar	potatoes	Cloves	Dried bananas	
Brown sugar	Lentils	Ground oregano	Powdered eggs	
Honey	Pearled barley	Dried basil	Cocoa powder	
Yeast	TVP	Italian seasoning	Cheese powder	
Powdered milk	Dried soy beans	Poultry seasoning	Egg noodles	
Dried Beans	Dried onions	Cajun seasoning	Corn meal	
Dried split green	Garlic powder	Dried parsley	Grits	
peas	Cinnamon	Pepper	Vinegar (use for pre-	
Black eyed peas	Baking powder	Curry powder	serving and cleaning	
Rice	Baking soda	Thyme	too)	

Food Storage and Good, Better, Best cont.

Add these food items to make all the "Better" recipe versions:

White flour
Butter flavored shortening
Regular evaporated milk
Butter powder
Crushed red pepper
Celery salt
Imitation bacon bits
Brown gravy mix

Then add these foods to make all the "Best" recipe versions:

Powdered sugar
Walnuts
Raisins
Chocolate chips
Coconut
Mapleine
Non dairy creamer
Salsa/taco sauce
Catsup
Onion soup mix
Dried chives

Dry mustard
Liquid smoke
Canned peaches, etc.
Canned crushed pineapple
Canned baby shrimp
Seeds:pumpkin, sesame, sunflower
Freeze dried ham
Freeze dried bacon
Freeze dried cheddar cheese
Grated Parmesan cheese
Spam

As stated before, these items are what we used to make all the recipes. You may have different tastes, so store what you like and adapt the recipes. You will now have a better idea as to what you should be storing. Just remember, what good does it do to have hundreds of pounds of stored food if your family won't eat it, or you don't know how to prepare it?

Planning Ahead

This part of cooking can be the most fun and the most important. As you look forward to cooking your meals you need to be careful and plan so everything goes together. What I mean is, if you want French toast or sandwiches, you need to make sure you have bread that was cooked ahead of time. Also as you plan think about conserving fuel. One way is by stacking your ovens, by doing this you use less charcoal while cooking several items at the same time. Another way, once your oven is already heated up you can cook several items one after the other such as biscuits, rolls, or cookies. Who knows what the circumstances will be if the power is out for a long period of time. Just remember to conserve your fuel.

By making a one week planner you will get a very good idea as to how much charcoal you will want to store and also what types of foods you really want to fix. As you practice cooking some of these meals, you will get a better understanding of what you need in your storage and how much. I included this section in the book just to get you thinking about how well you want to eat.

Each meal needs a little thought behind it. This type of cooking takes a little more time to prepare, like the beans and some of the pasta you need to soak for awhile or even overnight. You just can't all of a sudden say, "Hey, I want some Chili beans" and have them just like that. You need to plan your meals. We have made a simple planner so you can see what we mean. Please use this as a guide and make the meals you like. After you have a planner it is easy to decide how much you need for six months or even a year. Of course you will not want to eat the same meals week after week, so make sure you change your plans so you can have a good variety. Or you may end up eating noodle juice!!!

On the next page is a one week sample of recipes:

Example MEAL PLAN

	Sunday	Monday	Tuesday	Wednesday	Thursday	Friday	Saturday
Breakfast	Soak wheat the night before. *Whole Wheat Cereal* Cook extra to add to *3 Bean Salad*-Tues dinner.	*Hash browns and Eggs* Cook 4 cups Pinto Beans. Reserve ½ cooked beans for *3 Bean Salad* and *Refried Beans* for dinner	Mix bread dough before making pancakes. Make 3x's recipe for 2 loaves + *Cinnamon Rolls* *Pancakes*	Before cooking breakfast-soak apples for *Apple Pie*-bake using hot coals from breakfast *Oatmeal Cinnamon Rolls* (leftovers)	*Potatoes and Eggs* *Spam* *Onion Bread* (leftovers)	Mix bread dough to make 2 loaves-bake using hot coals from breakfast. *Cracked Wheat Cereal*	Soak apples for *Applesauce*-cook with coals from breakfast. *French Toast* (Bread from Friday)
Lunch	*Macaroni & Cheese* Cook dessert for dinner with the hot coals from lunch.	Chili	*PB & J Sandwiches* Made w/fresh baked bread from the morning.	Mix *Onion Bread* dough-bake using coals from lunch. *Clam Chowder Bread* (from yesterday)	*Split Pea Soup Cornbread* Cook cornbread stacked on top of soup.	*PB &Honey Sandwiches* Make *Brownies* for a snack.	*Chicken Noodle Soup Applesauce Bread* (leftover) Bake *Banana Bread* with hot coals from soup.
Dinner	*Chicken & Dumplings Chocolate Cake* Soak 4 cups dried beans for tomorrow.	*Tortillas Tacos*-TVP *Refried Beans 3 Bean Salad* Soak cracked wheat for dinner tomorrow.	*Wheat Loaf Corn Fritters Cinnamon Rolls*	*Spaghetti Onion Bread 3 Bean Salad* (leftovers) *Apple Pie* Soak split peas for Thursday's soup.	*Beef Pot Pie Apple Pie* (leftovers)	*Vegetable Stew Bread Rice Pudding* Cook pudding using coals from stew.	*Salmon Fish Patties Rice and Pasta Applesauce Banana Bread*

Planning Ahead cont.

Not only is this a meal planner but it will also help you plan your prep work. Pancakes, do I need to grind flour? Cereal, do I need to soak the wheat over night so it doesn't take so long to cook? What size oven should I use? How many ovens do I need? Where am I going to do the cooking? You don't want to be doing all of this just before you decide to eat. These are some of the things you need to plan on and do the day before.

How much should you cook? Just remember that if you are cooking meals out of this book and using charcoal as a source of heat, you probably don't have any power at all. Well that means more than likely the fridge is not working. Now the big question. What do I do with leftovers? The big answer is don't make any. Gosh, that's as simple as it gets. This is another reason you need to practice cooking, so you will know how much to fix and not have anything left over. You will be surprised how filling these dishes are.

Remember, if it needs refrigeration, you don't want to make more than you can eat. If you do, you may make yourself sick or get a good case of the trots. Not good. Be careful. Archie had an experience with spoiled food on an overnight scout campout with a bunch of guys and only one toilet. Let me tell you that is something you don't need at anytime, let alone when the power and water aren't working.

Just use good food handling practices. If you ever question if it's good….throw it out…don't take a chance. This is why you want to make the right amounts of whatever you are cooking. Wasted food is not easy to replace.

Oil

You need to have vegetable oil in your food storage. It is fairly inexpensive and will be used for everything you do with your Dutch oven. I prefer cooking with olive oil and it tastes great.   I use it all the time and rotate it. Storage time of all oils is one to two years in the house, not the garage or hot shed. So be careful how much you store. Shortening is good to store and is needed for your biscuits and desserts. Again, make sure you rotate it and use it as you go. Oil is one of those "you have to have" items. So you need to decide which type of oil you want. I would suggest maybe some of all of them, or at least the vegetable oil and shortening (don't forget butter flavored, it makes a good butter substitute when cooking).

Oil is a must for hash browns and other fried foods you may want to make, like apple fritters, fish patties, or scrambled eggs. You need plenty of vegetable oil for cooking with and for the maintenance of your Dutch ovens.

We love butter. Butter is the best. To have pancakes without butter is just unthinkable. There are ways to can butter at home. It will last up to 3 years, so if you are like us, you may want to have butter. Powdered butter in the #10 can is pretty good too. Our book is not about getting your food storage but how to cook what you have. We want to encourage you to store what you like to eat and hopefully you will enjoy learning to cook these items in your Dutch ovens with charcoal.

Cooking in your Dutch Oven

When cooking in your Dutch oven it must be on a flat surface clear of dried weeds, grass, or other combustibles, etc. This is where a Dutch oven table is nice but not necessary. After the briquettes are hot, then what? Coals are ready to use when they have a white ash on part of them. You will need to place the hot coals evenly spaced around in a circle the size of the Dutch oven. Place the top coals evenly spaced on the lid. Use the tongs to do this. See drawing below.

Each recipe tells you how many briquettes to use. The basic rule is: If it is a 10" oven, use 20 coals, 12" oven use 24 coals, etc. Just double the diameter of your oven and that is the amount of coals you will need to cook with. This equals about 350 degrees. For a cooler oven (like with granola) use fewer, for a hotter oven (like with rolls) use more. This is how you control the oven temperature. When baking you need twice as many coals on the top as you have on the bottom. This is because heat rises, therefore more heat is needed on the top. When cooking soups, all the coals go underneath. Sometimes you will start out with all of them underneath, then move some to the top. Each recipe tells you what to do. After practicing, you will know what to do and you won't have to think about it. However, different brands of briquettes produce different amounts of heat, so adjust the number of briquettes used accordingly.

Cooking in your Dutch Oven cont.

Use the Dutch oven to bake or boil in; use the lid as a griddle or to fry on.

Frying:
     You need to be very careful when you set up your oven lid for frying. Most foods fry very well at 375 to 380 degrees. You will want to measure the temperature for this if you have a temperature gun or just experiment with the coals and write down on the recipe how many coals worked best. In most ovens the curve of the lid is perfect for holding an 1/8" of oil to fry in. Do not put water into the oil. This will cause a real problem. Just be cautious. Frying hash browns and fritters are a real treat. Set the lid up on bricks, about 2" off the ground or a cooking table. We do not recommend using rocks. Regulate the temperature by adding or subtracting coals. Remember always use caution and safe methods when cooking with a Dutch oven.

Cooking in your Dutch Oven cont.

Griddle:

Use your lid as a griddle. Set it up just like you do for frying. This works well for pancakes, French toast and tortillas. You will need to lightly oil the lid until it becomes well seasoned and things don't stick. A metal spatula works best.

Boiling and pot cooking:

You will see how easy this works. It takes about 25 minutes to get a fair amount of water to a boil. With this you will want your coals under the bottom of the oven. When cooking something you will be stirring, such as soup, chili, hot cereal, etc., be sure the oven is firmly on the ground or cooking table with the right amount of coals underneath.

Baking:

This is the best. I love using it this way and I think you will too. Use the Dutch oven like the oven in your home. You can put in pans of biscuits or bread; casserole dishes and pie plates and any other baking dish you are used to using. We have found some advantages to this. If you are cooking for 1 or 2 people you can use the larger ovens to make small servings. Also, the baking dishes are easier to clean. We also found by using pieces of 3/8" re-bar or a ring of aluminum foil between the dish bottom and the oven there is less of a chance for your foods to burn on the bottom. See "How to make a foil ring" on the next page.

Cooking in your Dutch Oven cont.

How to make a foil ring:

Take 8" of foil, roll it up like a snake, shape into a circle, flatten slightly and there you are, a baking rack for your Dutch oven.

Foil Ring

Stack Cooking

You will find baking will require hotter temperatures on the lid and not as much on the bottom, as we explained previously. As you bake you will learn by experience the amount of charcoal needed on the top and on the bottom. It will become second nature to you. Also, if cooking more than one item at the same time, remember, stack the ovens. This saves charcoal and works great. (See picture above). One of the things you need to be careful of is some people have a tendency to keep opening up the oven to look at what is cooking. You will never burn anything this way but it's also hard to get it cooked. You have to let the oven heat up to do its thing. Most of the time you can let it go 15 to 20 minutes without looking. If you bake directly in the bottom, like Upside Down Cake or Cobbler, it works best to line the Dutch oven with foil before starting. This makes a big difference when it comes to clean-up.

Cooking in your Dutch Oven cont.

Things to remember:

- Don't make this hard.
- You really can't mess anything up.
- Don't worry about making things perfect. It seems like we are always able to eat what we cook.
- Have fun! Don't be afraid to make changes. Again, fix things the way you like them. After all, you will be eating it.
- Don't worry about starting up and lighting too much charcoal.   It's harder to get some going in the middle of cooking a meal. Remember, you can always put it out.
- Practice and get comfortable making meals.   Don't be afraid. When it's time to feed your family and friends, you'll be ready. You might just be the hit of the neighborhood.
- I have found its better to cook slower than real hot and burn stuff. Cooking with charcoal is not like your stove or oven. You don't turn a knob and it increases or decreases your heat source. When you add charcoal it takes a little while to get the results you were looking for. You'll need to watch it as it may get a lot hotter than you expected. As you cook more and more you will learn what works and how. Once you see how easy it is you can make all kinds of things.
- You don't need to worry about how to fix all that dried food. You are on your way to being able to cook your food storage without gas or electricity!

Conclusion

The purpose of this book has been to head you down the road of food storage cooking. We hope you are excited about making this a fun experience as well as part of your life. We have provided recipes for many dishes and as you try some of these dishes, we hope you take the liberties to add to or remove any ingredients you desire. These recipes were prepared with several thoughts in mind. The first is, how to use the basic items in your food storage to prepare delicious meals, and second, how to cook them using charcoal as a fuel with your Dutch oven.

We hope you find these recipes fun and easy to make and that your whole family will enjoy different things to eat. If you already Dutch oven cook, then try these recipes in your kitchen to see which ones you like and what extra foods you want to store. We never know when we might need to use our food storage.

Please send us an email. We would love to hear from you. Let us know how things have turned out or if you have any questions.

justdutchit@yahoo.com

If you would like to order more books please visit us at our web site:

www.JustDutchIt.com
or call
1-888-340-8947

BREAKFAST

Whole Wheat Pancakes
Whole Wheat Cereal
Cracked Wheat Cereal
Hash Browns
Potatoes and Eggs
Biscuits and Gravy
Oatmeal or Grits
Granola
French Toast

Breakfast

You can fix any combination of the above recipes for your meals. The main thing is understanding how to cook with charcoal.

Growing up as a kid I remember waking up in the morning and my mother would have breakfast ready for all of us boys. She would make things that would stick with you all day.   It was great. Following that same tradition my wife and I and all the 8 kids plus foster kids always started the day off with a big breakfast. As we prepared for our food storage we pondered over what to store so we could keep up the tradition of a big breakfast with good variety.

Guess what? It's easy and fun too. You can take the food storage items from your basic list and have great food. Then, with a few additional items go right from good to better to best. With the right planning you will have great breakfasts and a happy family.

Whole Wheat Pancakes

Use the lid of a Dutch oven, upside down, any size, propped up on bricks. 10 + briquettes under lid; makes 8 to 10

Good: Yes, I mean very good-whoa I like these!
*1 cup milk (1/3 c powdered milk
    with water to make 1 cup)
2 Tbsp. oil plus oil for lid
1 cup whole wheat flour
1/2 tsp. salt
1/2 tsp. baking soda
1 tsp. baking powder
1 Tbsp. sugar*

Directions:
Start heating lid before mixing. Whip together milk and oil. Mix together remaining ingredients, then add liquid. Don't over beat. You may have to add some water, depending how thick you like your pancakes. Oil lid. Lid is ready when water dripped on it dances around. Cook one at a time, turning when bubbles form and edges are set. Eat with powdered sugar, jam, syrup, or honey.

Better:
Add 1 powdered egg to liquid mixture.
Best:
Spread with butter and maple syrup. If you have mapleine and sugar, make homemade syrup. Just boil 1 cup water, pour over 2 cups sugar and add 1/2 tsp. mapleine. Stir until sugar dissolves.

Note: I love pancakes. When my wife used to say she was going to make whole wheat pancakes all the kids and I would make faces and gag. Well, after making these pancakes, I can say you will be back for more! We now mix up a bunch of the dry mix at one time and use it for all the pancakes we make. It was a wonderful surprise as to how light and fluffy these guys are. (Seems like you could eat a dozen or more) Once you serve them to your family and friends you will be making them all the time. Yum...

Whole Wheat Cereal

Any size Dutch oven (10" works best for this amount)
20 briquettes: all on bottom to start
Cook about 45 to 60 min.; makes 5 cups

2 cups whole wheat kernels
1 tsp. salt
water

Directions:
Rinse wheat. Put wheat in bowl or other container. Add 4 cups water and soak overnight. Drain. Put wheat into Dutch oven and cover with 5 cups water and salt. Bring to a boil over all coals, stirring occationally. Cover and cook with 2/3 of the coals on top about 45 to 60 min. or until tender, stiring every 20 minutes.

Note: If water is scarce, use the water that you soaked the wheat in to cook with. When cooked use as hot cereal with milk and sugar, butter, etc. Also use in chili, salads, soups, tacos: wherever you want to stretch your ingredients. I like to combine it with an equal part of re-constituted plain TVP and add a little cinnamon and honey. You don't even need milk on it. Save the leftover water to make soup.

Cracked Wheat Cereal

8" or 10" Dutch oven; 20 briquettes
Cook 20 min.; makes 2 1/2 cups

> *1 cup cracked wheat*
> *2 cups water*
> *1/2 tsp. salt*

Note: Cracked wheat is very versatile. It cooks up quickly compared to whole wheat. Have it hot with milk and honey or sugar. Serve it cold with chopped vegetables in a salad, make it into a casserole, or use as a substitute for ground beef in tacos or chili.

Directions:

Soak cracked wheat 1 or more hours, in 1 1/2 cups of water, but not in Dutch oven. Pour into oven with salt and bring to a boil over all coals. After boiling, stir and cover, moving 2/3 of coals to top. Cook about 10 minutes or until tender. Stir. Remove from coals and let sit 10 minutes then serve. Add more water if necessary.

Hash Browns

10" or larger lid; 15 to 20 briquettes
Cook 5 to 10 min.; serves 4

2 cups dried shredded potatoes
2 cups water
1/2 tsp. salt
Oil

Directions:
    Cover potatoes and salt with water and soak overnight (not in Dutch oven). Drain, pat dry with towel, then fry in 1/8" oil on lid over medium high heat until golden; turn and cook as before. You may have to cook them in several batches depending on what size lid you are using.

Note: Hash browns make a great addition to your breakfast menu. I get tired of having cereal every morning so hash browns are a nice change. I have been making fresh hash browns for our children for years. People who eat them wonder why they are so crunchy and golden brown on the outside and creamy on the inside. Here's the secret: You must have hot oil in your pan, (375 degrees). This allows the potatoes to brown. Also make sure you rinse them well before cooking. This prevents the starches from making a sticky mess. (This is especially true with fresh potatoes). Cook them in patties, not one large lump. Serve lightly salted and/or with catsup if available.

Potatoes and Eggs

10" Dutch oven; 10 + briquettes on bottom only
Cook 25 min.; serves 4

Good:

> *2 cups dried sliced potatoes*
> *4 cups water*
> *4 reconstituted powdered eggs*
> *1 Tbsp. dried onion*
> *1/2 tsp. garlic powder*
> *Salt and pepper to taste*
> *1/3 cup oil*

Directions:

Soak potatoes in the 3 cups of water overnight, but not in the Dutch oven. Drain, reserve liquid for soup, etc. Also soak the onions separately, then drain, pressing out excess water. Heat the oil in the Dutch oven, being careful it's not smoking. Fry potatoes in hot oil turning every 1 to 2 minutes until potatoes are golden brown. Don't let the oven get too hot, or the potatoes will get brown before they cook. You may have to remove some of the briquettes. Add the onions, garlic, and salt and pepper just as the potatoes are starting to turn golden. When the potatoes are done whip up the eggs and pour over all, stirring until set. Be careful, these cook fast. Remove from coals and serve.

Better:

> *Add 1/2 tsp. dried parsley.*

Best:

> *Add cubed spam and heat with potatoes before*
> *adding eggs.*

Note: This is a great breakfast dish; something different than hot ceral. If you have freeze dried cheese, sprinkle some over the top after removing from coals; put on the lid for a few minutes to melt cheese before serving.

Biscuits and Gravy

2 Dutch ovens, 10" or 12", also 12" or 14"
2 round 8" or 9" cake pans
or bake in bottom of Dutch oven on foil
See recipe for briquette amounts; serves 5-6

Biscuits

Good:

> 3 cups white whole wheat flour
> 1 1/4 tsp. salt
> 1 1/2 Tbsp. baking powder
> 1/2 cup shortening
> 1 cup plus 2 Tbsp. reconstituted powdered
>   milk

Directions:

Pre-heat larger Dutch oven for 10 minutes with 10 - 12 briquettes on bottom and 12 – 16 on top, depending on size of oven.

Stir together flour, salt and baking powder. Add shortening; then cut in with pastry cutter or 2 knives, until mixture is the size of peas. Add milk. Stir until moistened. Turn out on to floured surface. Gently roll or press dough until 1/4" thick. Fold dough in half, then again. Roll out again until about 3/8" thick. Cut into 2 1/2" rounds with biscuit cutter or glass. Place into 2 greased 8" or 9" round cake pans. Be sure a foil baking ring is in bottom of oven. Place pan of biscuits in oven, replace lid, and bake for 10 minutes, then check. Biscuits are done when golden all over and when removed they are not doughy inside. Remove pan with pliers and bake second pan of biscuits.

Biscuits and Gravy cont.

Better:

>   *Use butter flavored shortening in place of shortening.*

Best:

>   *Use white flour in place of whole wheat.*

Gravy

Good:

>   *1/3 cup oil or shortening*
>   *1/3 cup white whole wheat flour*
>   *Salt and pepper to taste*
>   *3 cups reconstituted powdered milk*

Cook in 10" Dutch oven over 16 briquettes, or stack this Dutch oven on top of biscuit cooking oven, therefore you don't need more briquettes. Cook oil and flour over coals until bubbling, stirring with a whisk. Whisk in milk and salt and pepper. Continue stirring until mixture thickens and comes to a boil. Remove from heat. Serve over hot biscuits.

Better:

>   *Use white flour.*

Best:

>   *Use butter instead of oil. (Add a little more if needed to absorb flour).*

Note: Biscuits and gravy are another one of those "stick to the ribs" breakfasts. Eat leftover biscuits with stew for dinner or as a snack with jam or honey.

---

*Be sure you use aluminum-free baking powder, such as "Rumford" brand, when making buscuits. If you use the less expensive baking power with biscuits you get a strange "baking powder" taste to them.

Oatmeal or Grits

10 inch Dutch oven, 14 briquettes on bottom to start a boil, then transfer 8 to top.
Cook 10 min.; serves 4-5

    2 cups water
    1 1/3 cups old fashioned rolled oats
     or 1/2 cup grits
    1/4 tsp. salt

Directions:

    Bring water and salt to a boil. Add oats/ grits and stir. Cover and simmer 10 minutes, stirring several times.

Note: Good old fashioned oatmeal or grits are part of my regular breakfast menu. As we used to tell the kids, "They stick to your ribs". If you have raisins, they are great in your oatmeal along with some brown sugar. Hot grits are good with a little bit of butter and salt and pepper, so be sure you have butter powder in your storage.

Granola

12" – 14" Dutch oven
18 briquettes: 6 on bottom, 12 on top
Cook 40 min.; makes 3 1/2 cups

Good:

*3 cups rolled oats (Quick or old fashioned. For
a higher protein cereal, substitute 1 cup plain
TVP for 1 cup oats)*
1/2 cup whole wheat flour
1/2 tsp. salt
3 Tbsp. oil
1/4 cup honey
2 Tbsp. brown sugar
2 Tbsp. water

Better:

*Add some type of seeds or nuts such as wal-
nuts, almonds, sesame seeds, sunflower seeds, flax
seeds, pumpkin seeds or coconut.*

Best:

Add 1/2 tsp. vanilla to liquids.
Add raisins or other dried fruit after cooking.

Directions:

Lightly coat bottom of oven with oil. Mix
together oats, salt, and flour in a bowl. Heat honey,
brown sugar, water, (vanilla) and oil in Dutch oven until
brown sugar is dissolved. Add dry ingredients and mix
until all flour is absorbed and everything is coated with
honey mixture. Pour into Dutch oven. Put on lid and
cook for 10 minutes. Remove lid and stir well. Replace lid, cook 10 more minutes and stir again. Cook
another 10 minutes, then remove from heat and stir
again and leave lid off. After granola is cooled, store in
air tight container.

Note: When the cold cereal is gone and you are tired of
cooked cereal, granola is a welcome alternative.

French Toast

Lid of Dutch oven, any size,
 propped up on bricks
10 + briquettes; serves 2

Good:

1/2 cup water
2 Tbsp. dry powdered milk
1/4 cup dry powdered egg
   (Double, triple, etc. the amount of
   ingredients depending on amount of bread
   being used.)
4 slices of bread
Oil

Directions:

Wisk together water and milk powder in bowl. Add powdered egg and wisk. Heat lid and coat with a little oil. Dip one slice of bread into mixture, turn over so both sides are wet. Place bread on lid and cook until golden, turn over (add a little oil) and cook until done. Be sure lid is not too hot. Add or subtract briquettes to regulate temperature.

Better:

Add 1/4 tsp. vanilla.

Best:

Sprinkle a little cinnamon into mixture.
Add non-dairy creamer to mixture.

Note: When baking bread make extra and plan to have French toast the next day.

Notes

LUNCH

Split Pea Soup
Potato Corn Chowder
Lentil Soup
Pasta
Clam Chowder
Macaroni and Cheese
Chicken Noodle Soup
Soy/Wheat Burgers
　　or Sausage Patties
Three Bean Salad
Bean Soup

Split Pea Soup

12" Dutch oven; serves 12. You can use a 10" if it has tall sides. 24 briquettes: 10 on bottom, 14 on top; Cook 60 to 90 min

Good:

> *3 cups dried green split peas*
> *5 cups water for cooking*
> *1 tsp. salt*
> *1/2 tsp . pepper*
> *1/4 cup dried onions*

Better:

> *Add 1/2 to 1 cup instant potatoes to thicken, if desired, after cooking.*

Best:

> *Add 2 Tbsp. imitation bacon bits before cooking.*

Directions: Sort out any small rocks (yes I said rocks), or deformed peas, rinse; then soak in 8 cups water at least 6-8 hours, but not in your Dutch oven. If you have plenty of water, rinse peas and drain, then add 5 cups water, with peas, in your Dutch oven. If not, then use the same water. Add salt, pepper, and onions. Put on lid and charcoal and cook 30 min. Stir and continue cooking and stiring every 20 min. after that.

Note: If your peas or dried beans are old, longer cooking may be necessary. This is one of my favorites. It's very filling, tastes great, and warms the soul. Adding the potatoes thickens the soup. Don't be afraid to try instant potatoes in other soups to add more body. I personally like thick soups.

Potato Corn Chowder

12" Dutch oven; 16-20 briquettes on bottom to start
Cook 10 to 20 min.; serves 8

Good:

1 cup dried or freeze dried corn or 1 can
1 cup broken dried potato slices
4 cups water
1 Tbsp. dried onion
1 tsp. garlic powder
1 1/2 tsp. salt
1/4 tsp. pepper
2 cups powdered milk, dry
4 cups more water for powdered milk
1/3 cup oil
3/4 cup whole wheat flour

Directions:

If using dried corn, (do not use dried hominy), soak it several hours or overnight, but not in the Dutch oven. Drain and save liquid. Soak potatoes and onions 1 hour. Drain, saving liquid. Add water to reserved liquids to make 4 cups in Dutch oven, along with corn and potatoes. (If using freeze dried corn follow label instructions. This and canned corn can be added the last 10 minutes of cooking). Bring to a boil over hot coals along with salt, pepper, and garlic. Remove some coals so mixture will simmer. Cook 10-20 minutes or until corn and potatoes are tender. Add back coals under oven. Mix powdered milk in 4 cups water, then add flour and oil, whisk until smooth. Add this to simmering chowder to thicken. Simmer about 10 more minutes.

Better:

Replace dry powdered milk with 1 can of regular
. *evaporated milk and reduce water by one cup.*
Use white flour instead of whole wheat flour.

Best:

Use butter in place of oil.

Note: There's nothing like warm chowder on a cold day. Add instant potatoes to thicken if desired.

Lentil Soup

12" Dutch oven; makes 8 cups
24 briquettes, start all on bottom

Good:

1 cup dry lentils, soaked overnight, at least 6
   hours, but not in Dutch oven
6 cups water
2 Tbsp. dried onions
2 to 3 Tbsp. dried carrots
1/8 tsp. dried oregano
1/4 tsp. thyme
1 1/2 tsp. salt
1/2 tsp. pepper
1/4 tsp. garlic powder
1 Tbsp. dried parsley
1/4 cup oil

Directions:

Soak lentils, then add the onions and carrots the last hour of soaking. Pour into cold Dutch oven; place on all coals and bring to boil. Cook with lid on to keep in heat. After coming to a boil add all other ingredients except oil. Remove 2/3 of coals from bottom and place on top to simmer. Cook 30 minutes or until lentils are tender. Add oil last 5 minutes of cooking.

Better:

Add 1 can of diced tomatoes.

Best:

Add 8 oz. of tomato sauce last 5 minutes of
   cooking.

Note: Adding the tomato products to this soup takes it over the top. If you don't have canned tomatoes or tomato sauce, I suggest you get some, you will be glad you did.

Pasta

10" or larger Dutch oven
20 briquettes on bottom for boiling
Cook 15 min.; serves 6-8

6 cups water
2 cups elbow macaroni or
    7 to 8 oz. spaghetti or any pasta
1 Tbsp. salt

Directions:

Bring water and salt to boil. Drop in pasta.
Heat to boiling then stir and boil for 8 minutes or until
done. Drain and use.

Note: What can you say about pasta? Make a salad by
adding Italian dressing and some canned olives. Or eat
hot with a white or tomato sauce. Of course it is good
with canned tomatoes or parmesan cheese.

Clam Chowder

10" Dutch oven or larger; 20 briquettes on bottom
Cook 30 min.; serves 8 to 10

Good:

1 1/2 cups broken dried potato slices
2 cups water
3 Tbsp. dried onion
1 tsp. garlic powder
1 1/2 tsp. salt
1/4 tsp. pepper
1/4 cup oil
1 1/2 cups powdered milk, dry
3+5 cups water
3/4 cup whole wheat flour
1 – 6.5 ounce can of clams, juice too

Directions:

Soak potatoes in the 2 cups of water 1 hour. Drain, saving liquid. Add water to reserved liquid to make 4 cups in Dutch oven, along with dried onion and potatoes. Bring to a boil over hot coals, then add salt, pepper, garlic and oil. Remove some coals so mixture will simmer. Cook 10 minutes or until potatoes are tender. Reconstitute powdered milk in a bowl with the 5 cups of water, then add flour and whisk until smooth. Add this to simmering vegetables to thicken. Stir. Add clams. Bring soup back up to a gentle boil for about 5 more minutes. You will have to add back the coals you removed to get the temperature up after adding flour mixture.

Better:

Add 1/4 cup dried celery to vegetables.
Replace whole wheat flour with white flour.

Best:

Use butter in place of oil.
Replace dry powdered milk with 1 can of regular evaporated milk and decrease water by one cup.

Note: We love clam chowder! Serve it with biscuits or bread and you have a meal. If you don't have clams just omit them and you have a great potato chowder.

Macaroni and Cheese

12" or larger Dutch oven; 20 briquettes on bottom for boiling; Cook 10 min.; serves 6

Good:

> *2 cups elbow macaroni*
> *4 cups water*
> *1/2 tsp. salt*
> *2 Tbsp. dried onion*
> *1 cup dry powdered milk*
> *2 tsp. oil*
> *2/3 cup cheese powder (Similar to that found in boxed macaroni and cheese. Buy it in the #10 can or in bulk section of some supermarkets).*

Directions:

Bring water and salt to boil. Drop in macaroni and onion. Heat to boiling, then stir and boil for 8 minutes.   Stir in dry milk and oil. After it has reconstituted, stir in cheese sauce. Your macaroni and cheese is ready to eat.

Better:

> *Use butter in place of oil.*

Best:

> *Top with 2-3 slices of bread torn into small pieces and browned by putting all coals on lid for about 10 minutes.*
> *Use freeze dried cheese instead of powdered cheese.*

Note: If you have powdered cheese, this dish is a real treat. Toss the bread crumbs with a little melted butter or butter flavored shortening along with a little dried parsley to make it special.

Chicken Noodle Soup

10" or larger Dutch oven
20-25 briquettes, all on bottom
Cook 30-40 min.; serves 6-8

Good:

> *6 cups water*
> *1 1/2 cups egg noodles*
> *1/2 tsp. garlic powder*
> *1 Tbsp. dried onion*
> *4 chicken bouillon cubes*
> *1 Tbsp. dried parsley*
> *1 tsp. salt*
> *1/4 tsp. pepper*
> *1/2 tsp. poultry seasoning*

Better:

> *Add 1 tsp. celery powder or 1 Tbsp. dried celery.*
> *Add 1 Tbsp. dried carrots.*

Best:

> *1 (12oz) can of chicken, with liquid.*

Note: This soup has lots of noodles. If you like more broth, just cut back on the noodles and add more water and bouillon. Enjoy this with a slice of whole wheat bread.

Directions:

Bring 6 cups of water to boil over all the briquettes in your Dutch oven. Add all ingredients, making sure chicken is broken up into pieces. When soup boils again remove half of coals and simmer for 12-15 minutes or until noodles are tender.

Soy/ Wheat Burgers or Sausage Patties

Lid of any Dutch oven propped up on bricks;
12 + briquettes under lid. Makes 8 patties.

1/2 cup plain TVP, soaked, then drained
1/2 cup cracked wheat, soaked, then drained
1 1/2Tbsp. dried onion, soaked and drained
Water
3 Tbsp. soy or Worcestershire sauce
1/2 tsp. salt
1/4 tsp. garlic powder
1/4 to1/2 cup whole wheat flour
Oil for frying

For sausage patties:

Add to the above a combination of rubbed sage, and black pepper, red pepper, and/or cayenne pepper. Just experiment as to how much of these you like.

Directions:

Cover TVP, cracked wheat, and onion with water in container and soak 30 minutes; drain. Mix all ingredients together, adding a little more flour or water as needed to bind ingredients together. Shape into 8 patties. Dip in flour. Fry on lid in a little oil over moderate heat. When golden brown turn over and brown other side. Serve on homemade hamburger buns with available condiments or serve plain.

Note: If any patties get overcooked, just steam them in foil with a little water over hot coals until warm and moist. These burgers are very nutritious. Also, try adding some dried vegetables which have been crushed, soaked, and drained. Also good cold.

Three Bean Salad

8-10 servings

2 cups cooked kidney or black beans
2 cups cooked pinto, navy or garbanzo beans
2 cups (one can) green beans, drained
   or use equivalent of reconstituted
   freeze-dried green beans
3 Tbsp. dried onion, soaked in water 30 minutes
   and drained
2/3 cup oil
2/3 cup sugar
2/3 cup vinegar

Note: If you have canned beans for all of the above, just rinse and drain all beans. This is Mom's recipe and is very good. Also, if you eat up all the beans and have juice left over, just add more beans and keep enjoying!

Directions:

Mix all ingredients together and store in covered container. Use up in a few days. Keep in coolest place possible.

Bean Soup

12" or larger Dutch oven
20-24 briquettes, all on bottom
Cook 1 + hours; serves 8-10

Good:

2 cups of mixed dried beans
(any combination of the following: pinto,
kidney, pink, great northern, black, white,
split pea, barley, lentil, blacked-eyed pea, red,
small navy).
Water for soaking and cooking
1 tsp. dried basil
1/2 tsp. pepper
1 tsp. garlic salt
1 Tbsp. dried parsley
1 beef bouillon cube
1 Tbsp. dried onion

Directions:

Rinse beans. Soak overnight (not in Dutch oven) in 4-6 cups water. Drain beans, then place them into Dutch oven and cover with 8 cups water (you can use some of the soaking water if needed). Add all the spices. Cover and bring to boil over all the briquettes. Remove 1/2 of the coals when the soup boils. Stir. Cover and simmer 1 hour or until beans are done.

Better:
Add 1/2 tsp. celery salt along with other spices
Best:
Add 1 - 15 oz. can of tomatoes during last 15
minutes of cooking.

Note: Add or remove whatever ingredients you want to suit your tastes. This soup is good with cornbread or biscuits.

Notes

DINNER

Scalloped Potatoes
Tacos
Cajun Rice
Black Eyed Peas
Dried Beans
Vegetable Stew
Au Gratin Potatoes
Tuna Cassarole
Spaghetti
Baked Beans
Beef Pot Pie
Chicken Pot Pie
Chicken and Dumplings
Whole Wheat Chili
Rice
Rice and Pasta
Mashed Potato Pancakes
Wheat Loaf
Fish Patties
Chili
Curried Lentils and Rice
Green Bean Mashed Potato Cassarole

Scalloped Potatoes

12" oven with 9" glass 2 qt. casserole dish. You can also use 10" oven without dish.
24 briquettes: 8 bottom, 16 top. Cook for 60 min.

Good:

3 cups dried potato slices
2 Tbsp. dried onion
3 Tbsp. whole wheat flour
1 cup powdered milk in 3 cups water
3 Tbsp. oil
1/4 tsp. garlic powder
Salt and pepper to taste

Directions:

Soak potatoes in salted (1/2tsp.) water for 1 hour. Drain (save water for mixing with milk). Grease casserole or line Dutch oven with foil. Put potatoes into bowel along with salt, pepper and onion. Mix milk and water. Whisk in flour. Whisk in oil. Pour over potatoes. Mix everything together and pour into casserole dish or Dutch oven. Bake, checking and stirring every 15 minutes.

Be sure bottom does not burn. It would be best to make a foil ring to set casserole dish on.

Better:

Use white flour in place of whole wheat

Best:

Replace powdered milk with 1/2 can evaporated milk.

Note: This is a basic recipe. If you have canned ham or Spam, cut up to make 1 cup of chunks and mix in with potatoes for a complete meal. If you have dried or canned peas these go great with scalloped potatoes. **Notice in picture below the casserole dish in the oven is on a foil ring to keep it off the bottom.**

Tacos

8" or larger Dutch oven
20 briquettes, all on bottom
Serves 6

Good:

10 to 12 corn tortillas, see page 107
2 cups boiling water
2 beef bouillon cubes
1 2/3 cups plain TVP
2 tsp. dried onion
1 tsp. chili powder
1/2 tsp. corn starch
1/2 tsp. garlic powder
1/4 tsp. ground oregano
1/2 tsp. ground cumin
1/8 tsp. pepper

Directions:

Bring the water to boil in your Dutch oven, then add the bouillon cubes making sure they dissolve before adding anything else. Add the onion and TVP, stirring to mix well. Put on lid. Set oven off the coals for 10 minutes to let the TVP steep. Mix all the spices together in a small bowl, then add to TVP. Return Dutch oven to coals and stir for a few minutes to heat through. If it seems a little dry, just add a small amount of water. Your taco filling is ready to enjoy.

Better:

Fix refried beans or rice too.
Also use 1/2 tsp. crushed red pepper.

Best:

Serve tacos with canned salsa or taco sauce.
Add any of your regular taco condiments.

Note: If you do not have TVP you can use 1 cup of cracked wheat cooked in 2 cups water with the bouillon cubes. Be sure to soak it first to cut down on cooking time. (See Cracked Wheat recipe) This is really good! Our daughter had to choose between ground beef taco filling or TVP filling and she chose the TVP.

Cajun Rice

8" or larger Dutch oven; 12 briquettes, bottom only.
Serves 5

Good:

> *2 cups hot, cooked brown or white rice*
> *Salt and pepper to taste*
> *3 Tbsp. dried onion, soaked in water 15 min.*
> * and drained*
> *1/4 cup oil*
> *Cajun spice to taste*
> *1 to 2 tsp. dried parsley flakes*

Directions:

Cook 1 cup rice according to directions in Rice recipe. While hot add salt, pepper, and onions. Pour oil over the rice. Sprinkle with Cajun spice and parsley; toss to blend. Add 2 Tbsp. of the onion water from soaking and heat for 10 min. Serve.

Better:

> *Dried green bell pepper, soaked along with*
> * onion and drained.*

Best:

> *One can baby shrimp*

Note: Rice is such a versatile food. If you don't like Cajun spice use Mexican, East Indian or anything else you want. Just be sure you have a variety of spices stored. Plain old rice can get boring day after day. Experiment.

Black Eyed Peas

10" oven or larger,   24 briquettes to start: 10 on bottom, 14 on top. Cook 1 ½ - 2 hours; serves 8

Good:

2 cups dried black eyed peas
2 tsp. salt
2 Tbsp. dried onions
Water

Better:

Add 1/2 tsp. garlic powder.
Add 1/4 tsp. pepper.

Best:

Add imitation bacon bits .

Directions:

Sort out any small rocks or deformed peas, rinse, then soak in 6 cups water at least 6-8 hours (do not soak in the Dutch oven). If you have plenty of water, rinse peas and drain, then add 4 cups water, with peas in your Dutch oven.   If not, then use the same water. Add salt and onion. Place over all coals and bring to a boil. Stir, then move 14 briquettes to top and cook until tender, 1-2 hours, stirring occasionally.

Note: What a wonderful southern dish! When I was in Mississippi I was introduced to this dish as a main course for dinner. The people who served it were of meager means and they were very proud of their dinner. We also had cornbread and greens. Very tasty, easy to fix, and very filling.

Dried Beans

10" Dutch oven, 20 briquettes: 8 on bottom, 12 on top
(You will need to add more during cooking)
Makes 5 cups

> *2 cups dried beans: pinto, red, kidney,*
> *black, white or navy*
> *2 tsp. salt (add after soaking*
> *and before cooking)*

Note: Take time when cooking your beans. You don't want a rolling boil, just a simmer. Use pintos mashed as refried beans in burritos; make the Baked Beans, Three Bean Salad, or use in the Chili recipe. Be creative and enjoy your beans.

Directions:

Sort out any small rocks (yes I said rocks, you never know what you might get) or deformed beans. Wash and cover with cold water and soak overnight (do not soak in the Dutch oven). Add enough water to cover; add salt. Cook covered until tender, 1 to 4 hours, depending on the beans. Fresh beans cook in 1 to 2 hours. Very old beans take a lot longer. Check beans for doneness after each hour. When done, drain beans (save bean liquid for making soup). Use beans as desired.

Vegetable Stew

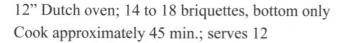

12" Dutch oven; 14 to 18 briquettes, bottom only
Cook approximately 45 min.; serves 12

Good:

> *1 cup dry green split peas*
> *1/2 cup dry pearled barley or 1 cup cooked*
> *   wheat (add wheat at the end of cooking)*
> *1 Tbsp. oil*
> *1/4 cup dried onions*
> *1/4 cup dried celery*
> *1/2 cup dried carrots*
> *8 cups water*
> *1 tsp. salt*
> *1/4 tsp. pepper*
> *1 tsp. Italian seasoning*
> *1/2 tsp. garlic powder*

Directions:

Soak peas, barley, and dry vegetables in the 8 cups of water at least 2 hours or overnight (do not do this in your Dutch oven). After soaking put this in Dutch oven and bring to a boil. If you cover it, it will come to a boil quicker. When boiling leave uncovered and gently boil for 30 minutes. Stir occasionally. Add remaining ingredients and simmer stew 15 minutes longer.

Better:

> *Add 8 ounces tomato sauce and 1 can of diced*
> *   tomatoes for last 15 minutes of cooking.*

Best:

> *Add 1 1/2 cups of dried sliced potatoes soaked*
> *   over night and then cut into smaller pieces.*

Note: One thinks, "How can a stew be good to eat without beef in it?" Well, this stew will lead the way on your top 10 list of stews, because it's really good!

Au Gratin Potatoes

12" Dutch oven with 9" glass casserole dish. You can use 10" oven without dish. 24 briquettes: 8 bottom, 16 top. Cook 1 hour; serves 8

Good:

     5 cups dried potatoes
     1 – 2 Tbsp. dried onion
     2 Tbsp. whole wheat flour
     3/4 cup powdered milk in 4 cups water
     2 Tbsp. oil
     Salt and pepper
     1/2 cup cheese powder
     1 cup crumbled bread crumbs

Directions:

     Soak potatoes for 1 hour. Drain (save water for mixing with milk). Grease casserole dish or line Dutch oven in foil and layer 1/2 of potatoes in bottom. Sprinkle with salt and pepper and 1/2 of onion and 1/2 of cheese powder.   Layer remaining potatoes, then salt, pepper, onion, and remaining cheese powder. Mix milk and water, whisk in flour. Whisk in oil. Pour over potatoes. Bake, checking every 15 minutes. On the 3rd checking, sprinkle bread crumbs over potatoes. Bake 15 more minutes. Be sure bottom does not burn. It would be best to make a foil ring to set casserole dish on.

Better:

     Replace dry powdered milk with evaporated milk and omit oil.

Best:

     Use 1 cup freeze dried grated cheddar cheese in place of cheese powder.

Note: To make a foil ring, take 8" of foil and roll it like a snake, about 1/2 inch thick. Then shape into a circle. Simple. Place at the bottom of Dutch oven to set dishes and baking pans on, making it more **like your kitchen oven.**

Tuna Casserole

(Chicken, Beef, or TVP works too)
12" or larger Dutch oven, 24 briquettes: 8 on bottom, 16 on top, Cook 45 min.; serves 6-8

Good:

2 cups egg noodles or other pasta
Garlic powder – dash or more
Onion powder or 1 tsp. dried onion (optional)
1/2 tsp. salt
1/4 tsp. pepper
1 can tuna or other meat (if using TVP use 3
  Tbsp. dry TVP and 1/3 cup more milk)
2 cups reconstituted powdered milk
1/4 cup whole wheat flour
1/4 cup oil
3 slices of bread, torn into small pieces for
  topping and tossed with a little garlic powder
  or other spices.

Directions:

Soak noodles or pasta in water for 15 minutes, drain. Grease 2 quart casserole dish. Put pasta in dish, then sprinkle, garlic, onion, salt and pepper, and tuna over pasta. Whisk flour into milk, then whisk in oil; pour mixture over all. Bake on foil ring for 30 minutes. Remove lid and stir, adding more milk if necessary. Spread bread crumbs over top of casserole. Replace lid and bake 15 more minutes, with most of coals on top so bread gets toasted.

Better:

Use white flour in place of whole wheat.

Best:

Replace oil with melted butter or butter flavored
  shortening.
Melt 2 Tbsp. butter or butter flavored
  shortening and toss with bread crumbs.

Note: I love tuna and noodles. This recipe is a one dish meal so it is made a little different than normal, but still very good. If you have peas they make a great addition to this meal.

Spaghetti

10" to 12" Dutch oven, 20 briquettes, all on bottom to start; serves 6-8

Good:

3/4 cup plain TVP or 1 cup cooked cracked wheat
1 cup boiling water
1 beef bouillon cube
3 – 8 oz. cans of tomato sauce or 2 cans of tomato
    paste and 1 can water
1 Tbsp. dried onion
1 1/2 tsp. salt
1 tsp. garlic powder
2 tsp. sugar
1 tsp. dried leaf basil
1/2 tsp. ground oregano
1 to 1 1/2 cups water
10 oz. dry spaghetti, broken into 3 to 4 inch pieces;
    or 2 1/2 cups elbow macaroni

Directions:

Bring the 1 cup of water to boil in your Dutch oven, then add the bouillon cube making sure it dissolves before adding the TVP. Stir. Put on lid and set oven off the coals for 10 minutes to let the TVP steep. Add tomato sauce and spices and stir. Set oven back over coals, then gradually add water and spaghetti or macaroni. Bring to a slow boil. Remove 1/2 of the coals to the top and cook for 15 to 20 minutes, stirring every 5 minutes and adding additional water if it becomes too dry.

Better:

Add 1 Tbsp. dried green bell pepper to sauce.
Replace 1 can of tomato sauce with 1 -15 oz. can of
    tomatoes, any variety.

Best:

Sprinkle Parmesan cheese over top after serving.

Note: You can substitute 1 – 24 oz. jar of spaghetti sauce for the tomato sauce and spices, but be sure you add the water since this is needed for the pasta to cook. Make garlic bread by brushing bread slices with a mixture of oil, garlic, and dried basil, oregano, or parsley flakes. When spaghetti is done invert lid over coals and when it is hot fry the bread, oil side down, until golden brown.

Baked Beans

10" tall or 12" regular Dutch oven
20 briquettes, all on bottom to start
Cook 2 hrs. or longer; serves 8

Good:

>2 1/2 cups navy beans (or any white, pink,
>   or soy beans)
>Water
>2 Tbsp. dried onion
>1 cup brown sugar (can use white sugar)
>2 tsp. salt
>1/4 tsp. pepper

Directions:

Pick through beans, removing any small rocks or imperfect beans; rinse. Soak (covered by 2" of water, but not in Dutch oven) overnight. Cook over 20 briquettes until boiling. Remove 2/3 to top and cook 30 minutes or until barely tender. Drain and add back 2 cups of bean water (being sure to save the rest so you can add more to beans while cooking if necessary). Add onion, sugar, salt and pepper and any other ingredients. Simmer 1 1/2 hours or until tender, adding more briquettes to keep beans simmering. Check every 1/2 hour to be sure beans aren't drying out.

Better:

>Add 2 Tbsp. imitation bacon bits when adding
>   salt and pepper.
>Also add 1 small can tomato paste or sauce.

Best:

>1 Tbsp. liquid smoke
>1 tsp. dry mustard
>1 small can crushed pineapple

Note: Baked beans are so good. When cooking the beans, be sure they don't cook at a rolling boil. You want a gentle simmer, so remove some coals if they are cooking too hot. Brown sugar is better than white if you have it. If you have bacon use it instead of bacon bits, adding bacon fat too.

Beef Pot Pie

2 Dutch ovens 12" or larger; 2 quart casserole dish;
serves 6-8
(If you don't have 2 ovens, use a pot from your kitchen,
raised up on bricks over the coals, for cooking the first
half of the recipe or carefully clean hot Dutch oven with
a small amount of warm water before baking pie. If you
don't have a casserole dish just leave it in the Dutch
oven, see note below)
24 briquettes: 8 on bottom, 16 on top

Good:

    2 cups dried potato slices, broken in half
    2 Tbsp. dried carrots
    1 Tbsp. dried onion
    1/2 tsp. salt
    2 1/2 cups water (for soaking the above)
    2 cups water (for cooking the vegetables; use
       above soaking water)
    3 beef bouillon cubes or 1 Tbsp. granulated beef
       bouillon
    1/3 cup fine whole wheat flour

    1 cup cold water
    1/2 tsp. garlic powder
    1 -12 oz. can of beef
    Pie crust pastry (see page 89)

Better:

    Replace whole wheat flour with white flour.

Best:

    Add 2 Tbsp. dried peas and/or celery.

Directions:

Soak the first 4 ingredients in the 2 ½ cups water for 30 minutes. Drain, then add water to the drained liquid to make 2 cups and pour into Dutch oven; place oven over all the coals. Put in vegetables and boil for 5 minutes. Remove vegetables with a slotted spoon, then dissolve bouillon in hot vegetable water. While that is dissolving, mix the 1 cup cold water with the 1/3 cup flour. Whisk until smooth. Add this to the hot liquid in the Dutch oven. Bring this to a boil, stirring until thickens. Add the canned beef, breaking into pieces. Stir and add vegetables, then stir. Remove from coals and make one recipe of the pie crust pastry. Roll out 2/3 of the pastry dough on floured surface. Fold over and carefully lift crust into casserole dish pushing it down to fit. Roll out remaining dough. Ladle beef mixture into dough lined casserole and then cover top with remaining pastry dough, trimming away excess and crimping edge. Cut 4 slits into top of crust, then carefully place casserole dish into 2nd Dutch oven on foil ring, then cover. Cook with 2/3 of coals on top for 35-45 minutes, or until crust is browned and juices are bubbling through slits.

Note: Be sure you don't put cold liquid into a hot oven; it could be damaged. If you don't have beef, make it with 1 cup cooked wheat or rice and use 2 more bouillon cubes to add more flavor and ¼ cup more water. Also, you can cook it directly in the Dutch oven if you don't have a casserole dish, just use pastry crust on the top only.

Chicken Pot Pie

12" Dutch oven; 30 briquettes: 20 on bottom to start, 10
on top; then 20 on top and 0 on bottom when browning
serves 8-10
Good:

> 2 Tbsp. dried onion
> 1 - 1 ½ cups of broken dried potato slices
> 3 Tbsp. dried carrots
> 2/3 cup oil or shortening
> 2/3 cup whole wheat flour
> 1 tsp. poultry seasoning, or thyme, sage, etc.
> 1/2 tsp. garlic, powder or granulated
> Salt and pepper to taste
> 6 cups water
> 8 chicken bouillon cubes
> 2 cups dry powdered milk
> 1 - 12 ounce can water packed chicken
> 2 cups whole wheat flour
> 1 Tbsp. baking powder
> 1 tsp. salt
> 1/3 cup shortening
> 3/4 cup reconstituted powdered milk

Chicken Pot Pie cont.

Directions:

Place potato pieces, carrots, and onion in container and soak covered with water about 20 minutes. Drain and reserve liquid. Put oven over hot coals. Heat oil or shortening, add 2/3 cup flour and whisk until bubbly. Add poultry seasoning, garlic, salt and pepper. In separate container dissolve bouillon cubes in 6 cups water (use reserved liquid from soaking veggies as part of this water); add the 2 cups of dry milk and stir. Add this to bubbly mixture in Dutch oven. Whisk until smooth; add vegetables and chicken (water too) and stir. At this point taste and see if any more seasonings are needed. In medium bowl, combine the 2 cups of flour, baking powder, and salt. Add shortening, cutting it in until small pieces are formed. Add the ¾ cup of milk and form into a ball. Turn out onto floured surface and press or roll into 12" circle or whatever size you need to cover pie ingredients in oven. Fold in half and carefully transfer to oven and place over mixture. Cut 4 - 2" slits into crust. Put on lid. Move all coals to top of oven. Cook about 20 minutes until crust is golden. Cooking time will depend on how hot the coals are.

Better:

Add some dried peas to vegetables.

Best:

Use white flour in place of whole wheat.
Replace oil with butter flavored shortening or butter.

Note: This recipe has a biscuit type crust. If you like, prepare a pastry crust instead. This will save your baking powder and powdered milk. You can also cook this in a casserole dish. Check to be sure the casserole dish fits into your Dutch oven and have a foil ring to set it on.

Chicken and Dumplings

10" or larger Dutch oven,
20 briquettes, all on bottom to start
Cook 45 minutes; serves 6

Good:

6 cups water
5 chicken bouillon cubes
1 Tbsp. dried carrots
1 Tbsp. dried onions
1/2 tsp. garlic powder
1/2 Tbsp. dried parsley
2 Tbsp. oil
1 cup dry milk powder
1 - 12 ounce can water packed chicken
3/4 cup water
1/2 cup flour

Directions:

Pour 3 cups water into Dutch oven and place over all coals. Add bouillon, carrots, onions, garlic, parsley, and oil. Bring to a gentle boil and cook 10 minutes (remove some of the coals so it doesn't boil too hard). Add flaked chicken, juice too. Mix together 3 cups water and the 1 cup dry powdered milk. Add to Dutch oven, stir. Add back removed coals. While waiting for this to boil again, mix together the 3/4 cup water and 1/2 cup flour. Mix well until all lumps are gone. Slowly pour this into boiling mixture, stirring to thicken. Bring back to a boil, then remove 14 coals to go on top of lid for cooking the dumplings. (You now want most of the heat on top)

Better:

Add 1/2 cup dried potatoes (shredded or broken slices) along with carrots.
Add 1/2 tsp. poultry seasoning or thyme along with garlic powder.

Best:

Add 1 Tbsp. dried celery.

Dumplings:

1 1/2 cups whole wheat or white flour
1/4 cup dry milk powder
1 1/2 tsp. baking powder
1/2 tsp. salt
1/2 tsp. sugar
3/4 cup water
2 Tbsp. oil

Directions:

Make dumplings by mixing flour, dry milk, baking powder, salt, and sugar in bowl. After these are mixed, add water and oil. Mixture will be sticky. Drop dumplings into bubbling mixture, making 12 dumplings. Replace lid with the 14 coals and cook 15 minutes. Dumplings are done when they are cooked through and are not doughy inside. Remove from coals and let sit for a few minutes before serving.

Note: You can have a hearty meal with very little effort just by having a few seasonings and dried vegetables in your storage. Adding the potatoes really takes this dish "over the top". Try looking for potatoes at a local market that carries bulk items.

Whole Wheat Chili

10" Dutch oven or larger
16 - 20 briquettes, all on bottom
Serves 6

Good:

> *4 cups cooked whole wheat (see whole wheat*
> *cereal recipe)*
> *1/2 cup dry TVP (optional); cover with water*
> *until softened, about 15 min.*
> *(Adding TVP makes it look like there is*
> *hamburger meat in your chili)*
> *2 Tbsp. dried onion*
> *2 Tbsp. chili powder*
> *1/2 tsp. cumin*
> *1/2 tsp. salt*
> *1 tsp. garlic powder*
> *2 Tbsp. oil*
> *16 oz. tomato sauce (add a little water if*
> *necessary)*

Directions:

> Combine all ingredients in Dutch oven. Cook
until heated through, 15 + minutes. Stir several times.

Better:

> *Add 1 Tbsp. sugar*
> *Add 1 tsp. crushed red pepper*

Best:

> *Add 1 can diced tomatoes*
> *Add 1-2 Tbsp. dried green pepper*

Note: If all you have to eat is whole wheat and some spices, then this chili will work for you. You will have to add some water if you don't have the tomato sauce. Or, to make a sauce, mix 2 Tbsp. flour and all the spices in a bowl. Whisk in 1 cup water. Stir this into wheat mixture. Mix up some biscuits or cornbread and stack cook your meal. (see "Cooking In Your Dutch Oven" section)

Rice

10" Dutch oven
24 briquettes: 8 on bottom, 16 on top
Makes 5 cups

Note: Rice is great for so many dishes. We have given you several recipes in this book, but the sky's the limit. If you have the ingredients, make your family's favorite rice dishes in the Dutch Oven.

Good:

4 1/2 cups water
2 cups rice
1 tsp. salt

Directions:

Place all ingredients into oven. Cook 20 minutes. Check and stir. If not done, cook 5 more minutes, adding water if needed.

Better:

Cook with 2 to 4 beef or chicken bouillon cubes dissolved in the water before adding the rice.

Green Bean Mashed Potato Casserole

10" or 12" Dutch oven; serves 8
20 to 24 briquettes, all on bottom to start

Good:

> *3 cups prepared mashed potatoes (follow*
> *   directions on can or package)*
> *2 cups water*
> *6 beef bouillon cubes or 2 Tbsp. beef soup*
> *   base (this is better than cubes)*
> *2/3 cup dry TVP*
> *1 Tbsp. dried onion*
> *2 cups water*
> *4 1/2 Tbsp. corn starch or 1/2 cup flour*
> *2 cans green beans, drained*

Directions:

Prepare mashed potatoes, then remove from Dutch oven to a bowl to be used as the topping. Wipe/rinse (using very little water) out Dutch oven. Return to coals and slowly add the first 2 cups of water.

When water boils add the bouillon cubes or soup base. Stir to mix, then mix in TVP and onion. As this mixture returns to a boil, whisk either the corn starch or the flour into second 2 cups of cool water. When that is mixed smooth, slowly add it to the TVP mixture, stirring until thick. Add green beans and stir until heated through. Dot top with prepared mashed potatoes and place lid on Dutch oven. Place 2/3 of coals on lid and warm about 10 minutes.

Better:

> *Replace 4 cups water, bouillon and corn*
> *   starch/flour with 3 cups prepared brown gravy*
> *   mix and prepare TVP with 1 cup*
> *   water and 1 beef bouillon cube.*

Best:

> *Replace TVP with 1 – 12 oz. can of beef, cut*
> *   into small pieces.*

Curried Lentils and Rice

10" Dutch oven; serves 6 to 8
20 briquettes, all on bottom; Cook 25 minutes

Good:

1/2 cup dry lentils
2 cups water
1/2 cup rice
1 Tbsp. dried carrots, crushed
1 Tbsp. dried onion
1/2 tsp. salt
1/4 tsp. pepper
1/2 tsp.. garlic powder
2 tsp. curry powder

Directions:

Rinse and drain lentils. Transfer to Dutch oven; add water. Bring to boil; reduce heat (remove 2/3 of the coals) and simmer, covered, 5 minutes. Stir in uncooked rice, salt, curry, pepper, garlic, carrots, and onions. Add back some of the coals. Cover and simmer 15 more minutes or until tender. Remove from coals.

Better:

Add 1 Tbsp. dried green bell pepper, soaked and drained, along with onions.

Best:

Add one can of diced tomatoes (draining most of the juice), after the 15 minutes, and keep simmering 5 more minutes, (add some of this juice to mixture if needed).

Note: If you like curry, this one is for you. Add or subtract any ingredients to make it just the way you like it. If you don't have lentils, just substitute cracked wheat.

Rice and Pasta

10" or larger Dutch oven; 15-20 briquettes
Cook 30 min.; serves 8

Good:

> *1/2 cup broken (about 1/2" long) pieces of*
> *vermicelli, angel hair pasta or spaghetti*
> *1 cup rice*
> *2 Tbsp. oil*
> *2 1/2 cups water*
> *4 chicken or beef bouillon cubes*
> *1/8 tsp. garlic powder*
> *Dash of pepper*

Better:

> *Add 1/2 tsp. dried parsley when adding garlic.*
> *Add 1/2 Tbsp. crushed dried carrots when*
> *adding garlic.*

Best:

> *Use butter flavored shortening or butter instead*
> *of oil.*

Directions:

> Pour oil into Dutch oven. Heat and add pasta and rice. Stir and cook until pasta is golden brown. Add water gradually, then add bouillon cubes and garlic. Cook and stir until it boils. Remove 1/2 of coals to lid and continue cooking until tender, about 20 minutes. Check and stir after 15 minutes.

Note: I made up this recipe when we had 8 kids to care for and they wanted lots of Rice-a-Roni, but we couldn't afford 3 boxes for one meal.

Caution! When adding the water to the hot Dutch oven, do so gradually. Adding large amounts of cold water to a hot Dutch oven can cause it to crack!

Mashed Potato Pancakes

Lid of Dutch oven, any size
15 – 20 briquettes, depending on oven lid size
Cook 10 min.; serves 6

Good:

>   2 cups mashed potatoes (reconstituted flakes or
>   potato pearls)
>   6 Tbsp. whole wheat flour
>   2 tsp. dried onion (soak, covered with water, 20
>   minutes, drain)
>   Salt and pepper
>   Oil for frying

Directions:

In bowl mix potatoes, flour, onion, salt and
pepper to taste. Heat lid. When hot (water drops dance
around) heat 1/8 inch oil, then drop heaping tablespoons
of mixture on lid (take back of spoon and flatten out
like a pancake) and fry until golden on bottom. Turn
and repeat for other side. Continue frying until all potato mixture is used. Serve as a side dish for dinner.

Better:

>   Add one lightly beaten reconstituted powdered
>   egg to mixture.
>   Add 1 tsp. dried parsley.

Best:

>   Add 2 Tbsp. dried or fresh chives.
>   Replace whole wheat flour with white flour.

Note: If you love mashed potatoes and onions, then
you will love these. They are somewhat fragile, so be
careful when cooking and serving.

Wheat Loaf

12" – 14" Dutch oven; 26 briquettes: 10 on bottom, 16 on top; Cook 1 hour; serves 6-8

Good:

> *1 cup uncooked cracked wheat*
> *2 Tbsp. dried onion*
> *3 beef bouillon cubes dissolved in 2 cups water*
> *3/4 cup reconstituted powdered milk*
> *3/4 cup quick oats (old fashioned is OK)*
> *1 Tbsp. oil*
> *1/2 tsp. garlic powder*
> *1/4 tsp. chili powder*
> *1/2 tsp. salt*
> *1/4 tsp. pepper*

Directions:

Soak cracked wheat and dried onion in bowl with bouillon water for 30 minutes. Add remaining ingredients and mix well. (The mixture will be very wet). Put in greased loaf or round cake pan. Place in Dutch oven on foil ring and bake for 1 hour. Remove from oven (I use long-handled pliers to do this) and let sit for about 10 minutes before serving.

Better:

> *Add 2 Tbsp. dried green bell pepper.*
> *Add 1/2 tsp. rubbed sage or Italian seasoning.*

Best:

> *Replace dried onion with 1 envelope dry onion soup mix.*
> *Serve with ketchup.*

Note: If the family likes meat loaf then this will be a good replacement for the "real" thing. You might want to make some beef flavored gravy by dissolving 2 beef bouillon cubes or 1 Tbsp. beef soup base (this is better than cubes) in 3/4 cup boiling water. Mix 1 Tbsp. corn starch or 2 Tbsp. flour in 1/4 cup water. Mix until all lumps are gone, then whisk into hot bouillon water. Heat and mix until thick and bubbly. Serve over loaf.

Fish Patties

10" or larger lid; 12 + briquettes
Serves 3

Good:

>*1 - 5 oz. can of tuna or 6 oz. can of salmon*
>*3/4 cup prepared mashed potatoes*
>*1 1/2 tsp. dried onion*
>*1/4 tsp. dried parsley*
>*1/8 tsp. garlic powder*
>*1/4 tsp. each salt and pepper*
>*1 + Tbsp. whole wheat flour*
>*Oil for frying*

Directions:

Drain and flake fish. Mix with mashed potatoes, onion, and seasonings. Mix in the flour. Heat Dutch oven lid with about 1/8 inch oil. Shape into 3 patties 1/2" thick. Heat oil on lid and when hot carefully place patties in hot oil and fry until golden brown. Turn and cook other side. Remove to a plate and serve.

Better:

>*Use white flour in place of whole wheat.*

Best:

>*Add 1 egg and increase flour to 3 Tbsp.*

Note: These are really good. Be careful the oil is not too hot! If you have some dill weed, try adding 1/4 tsp. along with the garlic powder. Enjoy!

Chili

10" Dutch oven
12 - 16 briquettes on bottom

Good:

    4 cups cooked beans (kidney, pinto, etc.)
    1 cup cooled bean cooking liquid or water
    2 Tbsp. flour
    1/2 tsp. garlic powder
    1/4 tsp. pepper
    salt to taste
    2 tsp. chili powder
    1/2 tsp. ground cumin
    2 Tbsp. dried onions, soaked 20 minutes

Better:

    1 - 2 Tbsp. dried green bell pepper.
    1/4 tsp. ground oregano.
    1/2 tsp. crushed dried red pepper.

Best:

    *Before adding flour mixture, add one can
    diced tomatoes and/or 8 ounces tomato sauce
    with 8oz. of water. Heat. Add 1/4 cup TVP,
    mix in and let simmer for 10 minutes, then add
    flour mixture. If it is too thick, add a little
    water.*

Directions:

    Mix flour and all spices in a bowl. Whisk in the 1 cup of water. Put beans, onion, and all other ingredients into Dutch oven. Heat. Add flour mixture. Heat through with coals on bottom. Be sure you bring it to a high enough heat to thicken chili gravy.

Note: Adding TVP to your chili will look like you have browned hamburger meat in it. You can use plain or beef flavored TVP. Be creative. Add corn, green beans or another type of beans in place of part of the beans called for in recipe. Serve with hot cornbread and you have a meal. Yum. Also, try heating your chili on top of the Dutch oven that has the cornbread cooking in it. Stacking ovens works great and saves on briquettes.

TVP is textured vegetable protein

Notes

Notes

Notes

DESSERT

Apple or Carrot Oatmeal Cookies
Brownies
Vanilla Cake
Apple Crisp
Dried Fruit Pie
Pie Crust Pastry
Apple Fritters
Apple Cake
Rice Pudding
Chocolate Cake
Peanut Butter Cookies
Cobbler
Upside-Down Cake
Applesauce

Apple or Carrot Oatmeal Cookies

12"-14" Dutch oven; 9" round cake pans; 24 briquettes:
8 on bottom, 16 on top (pre-heat 5 min.)
Cook 12 min.; 15+ min. for cookie bars
Makes 2 -2 1/2 dozen

Good:

1 cup whole wheat flour
1/2 cup honey
1 tsp. baking powder
1/2 cup oil or shortening
1/2 tsp. salt
1 cup rolled oats
*2/3 cup dried apple slices (broken into small
    pieces) or 2/3 cup dried carrots. Cover with
    water and soak 20 minutes, then drain, pressing
    out excess liquid*

Directions:

In large bowl mix together flour, baking powder, salt, and oats. Add apples or carrots. Mix together oil and honey. Add to dry ingredients. Drop onto greased cake pans, 7 per pan.

Better:

Add 3/4 tsp. cinnamon to dry ingredients.
Replace honey with brown sugar.
Add 1/2 tsp. vanilla.

Best:

Add 1 reconstituted powdered egg.
Replace whole wheat flour with white flour.
Add 1/2 cup chopped walnuts.

Note: You can divide dough in half and spread it into 2 cake pans to make cookie bars. Modify this recipe to fit your likes and available ingredients. Add raisins in place of apples, or omit cinnamon and add chocolate chips, etc. These are good broken in a bowl and served covered with milk.

Brownies

12" or larger Dutch oven; 8" square pan
24 briquettes, 8 on bottom, 16 on top (pre-heat 10 min)
Cook 20 minutes; makes 16 brownies
Good:

>   3 Tbsp. whole wheat flour
>   1/2 cup water
>   1 cup sugar
>   1/3 cup cocoa
>   1/4 cup oil
>   1/2 tsp. vanilla
>   3/4 cup whole wheat flour
>   1 tsp. baking powder
>   1/4 tsp. salt
>   1/4 cup water

Directions:

Cook 3 Tbsp. flour and the 1/2 cup water over coals in small pan if available. Cook and stir until it thickens. This happens quickly. Set aside until cool. In medium bowl mix sugar and cocoa. Add oil and vanilla and mix well. Add the 1/4 cup water to the cooled flour and water mixture then stir this into the sugar mixture.

Stir and add remaining dry ingredients. Mix well. Grease 8"x 8" pan. Pour brownie mixture into pan and place on foil ring in pre-heated Dutch oven. Cover and cook 20 to 30 min. Brownies are done when they pull away from sides of pan.

Better:

>   Replace all water with 2 reconstituted powdered
>   eggs and use 3/4 cup of flour only.

Best:

>   Add 1/2 cup chopped walnuts, raisins or
>   chocolate chips.

Note: Everyone loves Brownies, don't they? But without a mix and some eggs you are sunk. Well, not with this recipe. The only catch is you need to cook part of the flour with some water before you start making them. It would be best if you have a small sauce pan you can elevate over just a few coals. That way you aren't starting all of your briquettes and then letting them burn down while the flour/water mixture cools. Of course you can cook it in a Dutch oven and transfer the mixture to a small bowl to cool, then clean your oven to get it ready for the baking.

Vanilla Cake

12" or larger Dutch oven; 8" or 9" round or square pan 24 - 26 briquettes: 10 on bottom, 14 - 16 on top; Pre-heat oven 5 minutes; serves 9

Good:

> 1 2/3 cups whole wheat flour
> 1 cup sugar
> 1 tsp. baking soda
> 1/2 tsp. salt
> 1 Tbsp. vinegar (white or apple cider)
> 1 tsp. vanilla
> 1 cup water
> 1/3 cup oil

Directions:

Stir together the flour, sugar, baking soda and salt. Mix the vinegar, vanilla and water together and add to the dry ingredients. Add the oil and whisk until smooth and creamy, about one minute. Start your Dutch oven pre-heating now. Grease and flour pan, pour in batter. Place pan on foil ring and cook 20 - 30 minutes, (check after 20 min.). Cake is done when it pulls away from the sides of the pan and center is firm.

Better:

> *Use white flour in place of whole wheat flour.*

Best:

> *Use melted butter in place of oil.*
> *Dust top of cooked cake with powdered sugar*
> *or frost with favorite icing.*

Note: Like spice cake? Just add 1 tsp. cinnamon, 1/4 tsp. cloves, and a pinch of nutmeg. You can also add 1/2 cup of applesauce, or add 1/2 cup pumpkin and 1/2 tsp. ground ginger with the other spices for pumpkin cake. This is such a quick and easy cake, you will want to have it often. Serve with canned fruit for a special treat. It is very moist and like a pound cake. It keeps well because the vinegar acts as a preservative, delaying spoilage.

Apple Crisp

14" Dutch oven with 10" round glass casserole, or 10" Dutch oven; 24 briquettes: 8 on bottom, 16 on top (reduce number for 10"oven)   Cook 30 to 60 min. Serves 8

Good:

4 cups dried apple slices, soaked (cover with water and sit 1 hour) and drained (reserve liquid)
1/4 cup sugar
2 Tbsp. flour
1/2 tsp. cinnamon
1/8 tsp. nutmeg
1/4 tsp. salt

Directions:

After soaking and draining apple slices, mix the above dry ingredients together and stir into the apple slices with 3/4 cup reserved liquid. Put into greased casserole dish or directly on bottom on greased foil lined or greased Dutch oven. In another bowl, mix topping ingredients in the order they are listed, cutting in the shortening until small chunks form. Sprinkle over apples. Cover and bake 1/2 - 1 hour, depending on whether you are using a casserole dish (this takes longer) or directly in oven (lining with foil makes clean-up easy). Cook until topping is slightly browned.

Topping:

1 cup sugar
1 cup rolled oats (quick or regular)
1 tsp. cinnamon
2/3 cup whole wheat flour
2/3 cup shortening (butter flavored is best)

Better:

Replace sugar with brown sugar.

Best:

Use butter in place of shortening.

Note: You can use any dried or fresh fruit that you want. Just remember to soak dried fruit ahead of time.

Dried Fruit Pie

12" Dutch oven; 10" Dutch oven or a pot to cook filling,
24 briquettes: 18 to cook filling, then 8 on bottom,16 on top;
Pre-heat 5 min.; serves 8-10

Good:

> *1 unbaked 9" pie shell, trimmed to edge, and rolled*
> *out crust for top*
> *3 cups dried fruit: apricots, apples, raisins, peaches,*
> *etc. or combination*
> *2-3 cups water for soaking: soaking fruit 30 minutes*
> *will save on cooking time. Drain, reserving liquid.*
> *1 3/4 cup fruit liquid*
> *3/4 cup sugar*
> *2 Tbsp. corn starch or 1/4 cup flour*
> *1 tsp. cinnamon*
> *Dash of nutmeg*
> *1 Tbsp. shortening or oil*
> *Dash of salt*

Directions:

> Make pie crust pastry. Soak fruit 30 minutes.
Drain, saving liquid. Put fruit and 1 3/4 cup of saved liquid
into Dutch oven or pot on bed of coals and bring to boil,
stirring constantly. If using separate pot, support on bricks
so pot is not directly on coals. Mix spices with sugar and
cornstarch or flour and add to fruit. Stir until
dissolved and bubbling. Add fat and salt. Fruit should have
thickened. It will thicken more as the baked pie cools. Pour
hot mixture into pie shell. Moisten pie around edge with a
little water so top will stick better. Cover with top and trim
top crust 1" from rim of pan. Tuck top crust under bottom
crust around edge. Flute edge or use fork to seal edge together. Cut slits in top crust with sharp knife (4-6 slits,
1"long). Dampen top crust with a little water and sprinkle
on some sugar if desired. Place pie into Dutch oven
(pre-heated for 5 minutes) on rods or foil ring so pie is not
directly on bottom of oven. Bake approximately 40-50
minutes. Check after 30 minutes. If top is getting too
brown, cover with foil or remove some coals from top of
oven. Cook until juices bubble inside slits. Remove and
cool.

Better:

> *Use butter flavored shortening for fat.*

Best:

> *Use real butter for fat.*

> **Note:** This is one of the best surprises in the book. It's
> really good, especially the raisin/apricot pie. Yum!

Pie Crust Pastry

12" Dutch oven; 24 briquettes: 10 on bottom, 14 on top
8" or 9" pie pan; cook 5-10 min.; serves 8

For two-crust pie
2 cups whole wheat or white flour plus extra for
rolling
3/4 tsp. salt
1 Tbsp. sugar (optional)
3/4 cup shortening, oil, or lard (use 2/3 cup if
using oil or lard)
5-6 Tbsp. cold water

Directions:

Measure flour, salt and sugar into bowl. Cut in shortening, using two knives or pastry cutter. Sprinkle in water a little at a time, mixing until all flour is moistened and dough mostly sticks together (don't make sticky wet). You may need to add 1-2 teaspoons of additional water.

For double pie crust recipe: Divide in half. Put one half on lightly floured surface and gently flatten, shaping into flattened round. Roll out to two inches larger than inverted pie pan, gently turning and flouring underneath, being sure it does not stick to surface. When large enough fold in half and place in pie pan. Shape crust down into pie pan, then trim overhanging edge of pastry to 1/2 inch from rim of pan. Roll out top crust. Put filling into pie pan, moisten pastry edge around rim with water, then center top crust on pie. Trim top crust to 1" from rim. Tuck top crust under rim edge of bottom crust and flute or seal with fork marks around edge. Make 4-6 slits in top with sharp knife so steam can escape. Bake as directed in your favorite filled pie recipe.

For baked pie shell: Put rolled dough into pie pan. Trim bottom crust 1" from rim, turn under and flute edge. Poke holes in crust evenly all over sides and bottom. Bake in hot oven 5-10 minutes until golden. Be sure it is baked off the bottom of oven on a foil ring.

Apple Fritters

10" lid or larger; 15 - 20 briquettes
Cook 1 - 2 min. per side; makes 16 fritters

Good:

1 cup dried apples, broken into pieces
Water for soaking apples
1 1/4 cups whole wheat flour
1/4 tsp. salt
3 Tbsp. sugar
2 tsp. baking powder
1 1/2 Tbsp. corn starch
3/4 cup reconstituted powdered milk (use apple
 soaking water for all or part of the water)
Oil for frying

Directions:

Cover apple pieces with water and soak 30 minutes. Drain, reserving water for making the milk. In a medium size bowl, mix remaining ingredients in the order they are listed. Mix in drained apples. Heat about 1/8" oil on Dutch oven lid (or you can use any skillet you have, as long as it is up above the coals supported by bricks. Drop by tablespoon on to hot oil, being careful to be sure lid is not too hot. Fritters should be about ½" high and 2"- 3" in diameter. Cook on each side until golden, about 1-2 minutes. Remove cooked fritters to plate and continue cooking, adding oil when needed, until all batter is used.

Better:

Add 1/4 to 1/2 tsp. cinnamon before adding milk.

Best:

Sprinkle powdered sugar over warm fritters.

Note: Be sure you have powdered sugar in your storage to use on these yummy fritters. You can use other dried fruit as well: peaches, raisins, blueberries, etc.

Apple Cake

12" or larger Dutch oven; 24-26 briquettes: 10 on bottom, 14-16 on top; pre-heat 5-10 minutes; 8" greased square pan; Cook 45-60 min.; serves 9

Good:

>*1 1/2 cups dried apples, broken into 1/2"*
> *pieces (this equals 2 cups after soaking)*
>*2 cups water for soaking apples*
>*1 cup sugar*
>*1/3 cup oil*
>*1/2 tsp. vanilla*
>*3 Tbsp. water*
>*1 cup whole wheat flour*
>*1 tsp. baking powder*
>*1/2 tsp. baking soda*
>*1/2 tsp. salt*
>*1/2 tsp. cinnamon*
>*1/4 tsp. ground cloves*

Directions:

Soak apple pieces for 30 minutes. Drain and use this water when making cake. Grease and flour 8" square pan. In medium bowl cream together sugar, oil, vanilla and water. In separate bowl mix together all dry ingredients. Mix both parts together in larger of the 2 bowls. Add apples. Pour into square pan. Place into pre-heated Dutch oven on foil ring. Cover and cook being sure more than 1/2 of coals are on the top. Bake 45-60 minutes. Check it after 30 minutes, then every 10-15 minutes after that. Cake is done when the cake has pulled away from the pan sides.

Better:

>*Add 1 powdered egg to the 3 Tbsp. water.*
>*Replace whole wheat flour with white flour.*

Best:

>*Add 1/2 cup chopped walnuts.*
>*When done and still warm, make a glaze of 1/2*
> *cup powdered sugar, 1 Tbsp. water and*
> *1/4 tsp. vanilla.*

Note: This is a very moist cake, almost like an old fashioned pudding. It is my favorite cake for my birthday every year. I also like raisins in it. It is just about as good with whole wheat flour as it is with white. Be sure you have a pair of pliers to lift the cake pan out of the Dutch oven. Enjoy!

Rice Pudding

10" Dutch oven; 16 briquettes, bottom to start
Cook 1 - 2 hrs.; serves 8 - 10

Good:

> *1/2 cup rice*
> *1 cup water*
> *1/2 tsp. salt*
> *2/3 cup sugar*
> *3 Tbsp. oil*
> *1 quart (4 cups) reconstituted powdered milk*
> * (make it with an extra Tbsp. of milk powder)*

Directions:

Put water, rice, and salt in Dutch oven and bring to a boil. Cook and stir occasionally for 7 minutes, adding a little water if necessary. Add sugar, oil, and milk, stirring after each. Continue cooking and stirring 20-30 minutes until desired tenderness. Be sure pudding is gently boiling, not a hard rolling boil. For a creamier pudding cook with lid on and place 10 of the briquettes on top and cook 1 hour, stirring every 15 minutes.

Remove from heat. Remove lid and stir. Replace lid, remove all coals, and let sit for 30 minutes before serving.

Better:

> *Add 1/2 tsp. vanilla along with the milk.*

Best:

> *Replace oil with butter.*

Note: I couldn't get enough of this rice pudding when I first made it. It's very creamy. Sprinkle a little cinnamon on it for a special treat. It's great warm or cold; it's just good any time!

Chocolate Cake

12" Dutch oven; 8" or 9" round or square pan
24 - 26 briquettes: 10 on bottom, 14 - 16 on top; pre-heat oven 5 minutes; Cook 30 min.; serves 9

Good:

> 1 1/2 cups whole wheat flour
> 1 cup sugar
> 1/4 cup unsweetened cocoa
> 1 tsp. baking soda
> 1/2 tsp. salt
> 1 Tbsp. vinegar (white or apple cider)
> 2 tsp. vanilla
> 1 cup water
> 1/3 cup oil

Directions:

Stir together the flour, sugar, cocoa, baking soda and salt. Mix the vinegar, vanilla and water together and then add to the dry ingredients. Add the oil and mix well until smooth and creamy, about one minute. Grease and flour pan, pour batter in pan. Place pan on foil ring and cook around 30 minutes. (check after 20 minutes). Cake is done when it has pulled away from sides of pan.

Better:

> Use white flour in place of whole wheat.

Best:

> Use melted butter in place of oil.
> Dust top of cooked cake with powdered sugar.

Note: Do the kids love chocolate cake? Well you better have plenty of cocoa and vinegar stored because this cake is a favorite with children. Sift a little powdered sugar on top to finish it off.

Peanut Butter Cookies

12"-14" Dutch oven; 9" round cake pans, 24 briquettes:
8 on bottom, 16 on top (pre-heat 5 min.),
Cook 10 to 12 minutes; makes 2 dozen

Good:

1/4 cup reconstituted powdered milk
1/4 tsp. vinegar
1/2 cup shortening
1/2 cup creamy peanut butter
1/2 cup white sugar
1/2 cup brown sugar
1 1/4 cups whole wheat flour
1/2 tsp. baking powder
3/4 tsp. baking soda
1/4 tsp. salt

Directions:

Prepare the liquid powdered milk and pour the vinegar into it. Let sit for 5 minutes while you begin measuring the other ingredients.   In large bowl, mix the shortening, peanut butter, white sugar, brown sugar and milk mixture until smooth. Add the 4 remaining ingredients and mix until well blended. Drop onto greased cake pans, 7 per pan. Flatten with a fork that has been dipped in sugar, making a criss-cross pattern. Bake on foil ring 10 to 12 minutes. Use pliers to remove from oven.

Better:

Replace whole wheat flour with white flour.

Best:

Replace powdered milk and vinegar with 1 reconstituted powdered egg.

Note: These cookies are so good you can't tell they were made with no eggs. They are great just using the "Good" version.

Cobbler

10" or 12" Dutch oven, 24 briquettes: all on bottom to start, then 8 bottom, 16 top; Cook 30 to 60 min.; serves 10-12

Good:

> 3 - 5 cups dried fruit, soaked 1 hour; drain
> 1 cup sugar
> 3 Tbsp. corn starch
> 1 tsp. cinnamon (optional)
> 1 1/2 cups water (use water used to soak fruit)
> 1 cup whole wheat flour
> 1/2 - 1 cup sugar (depending on how sweet you want it)
> 1 1/2 tsp. baking powder
> 1/4 tsp. salt
> 1/4 cup oil
> 1/4 cup reconstituted powdered milk, ½ cup if making a cake-like batter

Directions:

Mix together sugar, corn starch and cinnamon in Dutch oven. Add water (use water fruit soaked in) and stir until sugar dissolves. Add drained fruit and cook and stir over coals until fruit is partly cooked and mixture is thick.
Make topping: Mix together flour, sugar, baking powder, and salt. Add oil and milk. Mix. Turn out on lightly floured surface and roll out to 1/2" thick or just press with hands. Cut into 1" strips and lay these over fruit mixture. If you want moister dough just add more milk until desired consistency (make either drop biscuits or add more milk to make a thick cake-like batter you would pour over fruit). Bake 30 minutes, then check. Cobbler is done when topping is golden and fruit is bubbly.

Better:

> Use canned fruit; drain first, saving 1 cup juice to mix with 2 Tbsp. cornstarch. Mix together sugar and cinnamon, then mix everything together in Dutch oven. Cover with topping.
> Use fresh fruit in place of dried.
> Replace whole wheat flour with white flour.

Best:

> Replace powdered milk with evaporated milk for a richer batter.
> Replace oil with melted butter.

Note: For easier clean-up, line oven with heavy duty foil. If you like nuts, sprinkle 1/2 cup chopped walnuts over fruit mixture and on top. Be careful it doesn't burn on bottom.

Upside-Down Cake

12"- 14" oven; 8" square pan
26 briquettes: 10 on bottom, 16 on top (pre-heat 5 min.), Cook 30 to 45 min; serves 9

Good:

> 1/4 cup butter flavored shortening
> 1/2 cup brown sugar
> Fruit: 1 1/2 cups dried apples, soaked 30 minutes and drained or 2 – 15 oz. cans of peaches, fruit cocktail, cherries, etc. drained. For pineapple use 2 short cans or 1 tall.
> 1 2/3 cups whole wheat flour
> 1 cup sugar
> 1 tsp. baking soda
> 1/2 tsp. salt
> 1 Tbsp. vinegar (white or apple cider)
> 1 Tbsp. vanilla
> 1 cup water
> 1/3 cup oil

Directions:

Melt the butter flavored shortening in the bottom of the square pan. Sprinkle brown sugar evenly over melted shortening. Drain fruit, then arrange fruit on top of brown sugar. Set pan aside. Start your Dutch oven pre-heating now.   Stir together the flour, sugar, baking soda and salt. Mix the vinegar, vanilla and water together and then add to the dry ingredients. Add the oil and whisk until smooth and creamy, about one minute. Pour cake batter over fruit. Place pan on foil ring and cook 30 to 45 minutes. (Check after 30 minutes). Cake is done when it has pulled away from sides of pan and center is firm. After removing from oven (use pliers to lift pan out of oven), cool 10 minutes, then take a knife and run it around edge of cake. Place a plate or small cookie sheet over top of cake, hold in place and turn up-side down. Leave the pan on the cake for a few minutes before removing.

Better:

Use white flour in place of whole wheat flour.

Best:

Use melted butter in place of butter flavored shortening.

Note: If you have a yellow or white packaged cake mix, fix it according to package directions. If you have no eggs, that's OK, just mix the juice you drained off your canned fruit with water and use ¼ cup more water than asked for on the box. You can use it in a foil lined 12" Dutch oven. Just double the amount of butter flavored shortening and brown sugar in bottom of oven. Double the amount of fruit (use 20 oz. can of pineapple if making pineapple cake). If you have nuts or maraschino cherries arrange them over fruit. Pour cake batter over all and place lid on Dutch oven. Bake as directed above.

Applesauce

Any size Dutch oven, depending on amount;
16 to 24 briquettes.
Cook 30 minutes; makes 1 1/2 cups

Good:

1 cup dried apple slices,
  broken into pieces, soaked
1 1/2 cups water

Directions:

Soak apple pieces in the water for 30 minutes. Pour apples and water into Dutch oven, place over coals, and cook 30 minutes, stirring often. Add more water if necessary to keep a moist consistency. Remove from coals and mash apples with a potato masher or put through a sieve. Serve warm or cold.

Better:

Add sugar to taste, after cooking.

Best:

Add cinnamon.

Note: Most kids love applesauce, so why not make some out of those dried apples you have. Nothing could be easier, and if you look in the bottom of the can, you'll find a bunch of small pieces, perfect for making your applesauce.

Notes

BREAD

Corn Bread
Whole Wheat Bread
Onion Bread
Tortillas
Scottish Oat Cakes
Dinner Rolls
Cinnamon Rolls
Banana Bread
Corn Fritters

Breads

I really enjoy cooking breads in the Dutch oven. Whatever bread you bake in your home oven, you can cook in your Dutch oven. There are several methods for baking your bread in the Dutch oven: 1) In your regular bread pans, 2) on foil, or 3) directly on the bottom of the Dutch oven. My preferred method is in my regular bread pans. You will need at least a 12" Dutch oven if using loaf pans. If you like a tall loaf, I recommend buying the 12" oven that is 5" deep instead of the regular 3 1/2" deep oven. A 10" oven is good for two mini loaf pans, 12" holds three and the 14" Dutch oven holds four mini pans. Dinner rolls work well in a round cake pan in the 10" or larger oven; if using a square pan you will need a 12" or larger Dutch oven. Forming your loaf into a round dome for baking on foil or in a cake pan works great too.

When baking bread, biscuits, cinnamon rolls, etc. it is best to pre-heat your oven for 5 to 10 minutes, just like you would when baking in your kitchen oven. Do this by putting 2/3 of the briquettes on the top and 1/3 under the bottom. If it is necessary to cook directly inside on the bottom of the Dutch oven, be sure you grease the bottom and sides of the oven before placing the dough into the oven to rise. You won't be able to pre-heat, so start the cooking when the dough hasn't quite risen double. Of course it will take another 10 minutes or so for your bread to cook when using this method. If cooking on foil, grease the foil before placing the dough on it. After it has risen, carefully lift the foil (have two people do this) into the pre-heated oven being careful not to burn yourself. I have found that the best way to bake bread is to put the pan on a foil ring, a baking rack or small rods, such as cut re-bar. This will help prevent burning the bottom of the bread. I say this because we have a tendency to put too many coals under the oven, thus burning what you are cooking. The baking ring simulates cooking in your kitchen oven. To make a foil ring, just tear off about 8" of foil, roll it into a snake, shape it into a ring and then smash it down to about 1/4" thick. There you have it, a baking rack, just perfect for bread pans, cake pans, and casserole dishes.

Breads cont.

Your bread is done when it is golden brown and sounds hollow when you thump it with your finger. I recommend having a pair of long handled pliers for lifting the pans out of the Dutch oven. VERY IMPORTANT! Go to the store tomorrow and buy a large container of yeast. Put it into your freezer and forget about it if you want. At least you will have your yeast and be able to bake bread when you need to. Or, use it and rotate it, but YOU NEED TO HAVE YEAST if you want to have bread to eat. Then think about what you want to eat on the bread, like peanut butter or jam, and have that in your storage as well. Have fun making your breads - you need to be sure and have the basic ingredients in your storage: flour (or wheat and a hand grinder; or an electric grinder and a generator with fuel), yeast, sweetener (honey or sugar), salt, oil (or other fat), and water. Also you will need shortening for greasing your pans.

We found it effective to plan on days to cook breads. If you make your bread ahead of time you can make several loaves and maximize your fuel. Depending on your needs, you may want one or two days a week to do breads. This is why it is good to know several days in advance what meals you will be preparing. Our whole wheat bread recipe makes one loaf and the dinner rolls make four round/square pans. Our recipes are meant to give you instructions on how to make bread if you are a beginner and then teach you how to bake it in your Dutch oven. If you are an experienced baker, just use your own recipes and use the Dutch oven techniques we mentioned. It's a good idea to try baking in your Dutch oven BEFORE you HAVE to. You won't be able to cook 6 loaves at a time like you do in your kitchen oven, so adjust your recipes as necessary. No matter what recipes you use, just have fun!

Corn Bread

12" Dutch oven or larger; 8" square pan; 24 briquettes: 8 on bottom, 16 on top (pre-heat 5 minutes); Cook 30 minutes; serves 9

Good:

> 1 1/3 cups cornmeal
> 1/4 cup vegetable oil
> 2/3 cup whole wheat flour
> 1 1/3 cups milk
> 1 1/2 tsp. baking powder
> 1/2 tsp. salt
> 1/3 cup sugar

Directions:

Grease 8" square pan. In medium bowl mix dry ingredients. Whisk oil and milk (and egg) together. Add to dry ingredients and mix. Pour into prepared pan, and then set down into pre-heated Dutch oven.

Better:

> *Replace whole wheat flour with white flour.*

Best:

> *Add 1 powdered egg to the milk and oil mixture.*

Note: You can double the recipe, then pour directly into Dutch oven which has been lined with foil. Be sure you grease the Dutch oven if cooking this way. If you line it with foil you will have an easy clean-up. However, by cooking directly in oven you get a crisper brown bottom and edges, almost crunchy; great stuff. By adding corn, canned green diced chilies, onions or other vegetables to the batter you can make great variations. Cold cornbread broken into a bowl with milk and a little sugar or honey over it knocks you off your chair; great southern treat.

This is really good!

Whole Wheat Bread

12" to 14" Dutch oven; 28 briquettes: 10 on bottom, 18 on top; (pre-heat 5 min.); makes 1 loaf
Cook 45 minutes

    1 cup warm water
    1 tsp. sugar
    1 1/2 tsp. yeast
    1 Tbsp. sugar or honey
    1 tsp. salt
    2 cups whole wheat flour
      (plus some flour for kneading)
      (use white flour for white bread)
    1 1/2 Tbsp. oil

HEY !!! POUR SOME HONEY ON THAT PUPPY!

Directions:

    Mix first 3 ingredients. Let sit for 5 minutes. Add oil, salt, honey, and 1 cup flour. Beat 2 minutes, then add remaining flour. Knead 10 minutes on floured surface, adding flour while kneading. Grease bowl, put dough into bowl, and then turn dough greased side up. Cover with cloth and let rise in warm place until double, 1 to 2 hours. Punch down, then form into loaf and put in greased 9 1/2" x 5 1/2" loaf pan. This larger pan works best because in a smaller pan the bread can rise too high and touch the lid. Let rise until double, about 1 hour. Start briquettes after 1/2 hour of rising. When coals are ready, place Dutch oven over 10 coals with lid on. Place remaining coals on top (this will pre-heat the oven). When bread has risen put it in Dutch oven on top of a foil ring and replace lid. Check bread after 30 minutes to be sure it is starting to brown and not cooking too fast. When done tap top crust and it should have a hollow sound. Remove from pan and cool on wire rack. While oven is hot, cook another loaf, cookies, or whatever you may be having later that day.

Onion Bread

12" to 14" Dutch oven; 28 briquettes: 10 on bottom, 18 on top (pre-heat 5 min.)
Cook 45 minutes; makes 1 loaf

Good:

> *1 cup warm water*
> *2 Tbsp. dried onion*
> *2 tsp. sugar*
> *1 1/2 tsp. yeast*
> *1 1/2 Tbsp. oil*
> *1 tsp. salt*
> *1 Tbsp. sugar or honey*
> *1 cup whole wheat flour*
> *2 cups fine whole wheat flour plus extra*

Directions:

Mix first 4 ingredients. Let sit for 5 minutes. Add oil, salt, sugar, and one cup of the flour and beat 2 minutes, then add remaining flour. Kneed 10 minutes on floured surface, adding flour while kneading. Grease bowl, put dough into bowl, and then turn dough greased side up. Cover with cloth and let rise in warm place until double, about 1 hour. Punch down, then form into loaf and put into greased loaf pan. Let rise until double, about 1 hour. Start briquettes after 1/2 hour of rising. When coals are ready, place Dutch oven over 10 coals with lid on. Place remaining coals on top (this will pre-heat the oven). When bread has risen put it in Dutch oven and replace lid. Check bread after 30 minutes to be sure it is starting to brown and not cooking too fast. When done tap top crust and it should have a hollow sound. Remove from pan and cool on wire rack. While oven is hot, cook another loaf, cookies, or whatever you may be having later that day.

Better:

> *Replace whole wheat flour with white flour.*

Best:

> *Use softened butter instead of oil.*

Note: This is a wonderful dinner bread. It is even better the next day since the onion flavor has time to totally permeate the loaf.

Tortillas

Lid of a Dutch oven, any size, propped up on bricks; 10 + briquettes; makes 10 - 7" tortillas

Flour tortillas:

> *2 cups whole wheat or white flour*
> *3/4 tsp. salt*
> *1 tsp. baking powder*
> *2 Tbsp. oil or shortening*
> *2/3 – 3/4 cup water*

Directions:

Measure dry ingredients into bowl. Stir with hands. Add oil or shortening. Mix with hands. Add water and knead until smooth, forming a smooth ball, adding more flour or water as needed. Let sit 20 min. You want it pliable but not too sticky. Form 10 balls of equal size. Cover with plastic wrap or damp towel so they don't dry out. Using a rolling pin, roll each portion on lightly floured surface until dough is a very thin circle. Cook on dry (no oil) medium hot lid until underside is dry, bubbly and lightly browned. Turn and cook other side. Put cooked tortillas on plate and cover with dish towel to keep warm and pliable.

Corn tortillas:

> *1 cup corn meal*
> *1 1/4 cups boiling water*
> *2 to 2 1/2 cups whole wheat or white flour*
> *1/2 tsp. salt*

Directions:

Pour boiling water over the corn meal. Let sit 10 min. Mix salt and flour together. Add enough of the flour to the corn meal mixture to make a kneadable dough. Knead 5 to 10 min. Let sit 5 min. Pinch off a piece of dough the size of a golf ball. Roll it out on a floured surface to make a 4" circle. Cook on an un-oiled lid about 2 min. on each side. If the tortilla sticks, sprinkle a little salt on the lid.

Note: We all like tortillas! Use them for tacos, burritos, or as a snack with cinnamon and sugar. If you're out of yeast they can be an alternate bread source.

Scottish Oat Cakes

Lid of any size oven; 8 - 10 briquettes underneath lid (not too hot) Cook 15 min.; makes 10 cakes

1 cup rolled oats, quick or old fashioned
1/2 cup flour
1-2 Tbsp. sugar
1/2 tsp. baking powder
1/4 tsp. salt
3 Tbsp. shortening or butter
1/3 to 1/2 cup water
Oil for cooking

Directions:

Combine in bowl all ingredients except shortening and water. Mash in fat with fork or fingers until crumbly. Stir in enough water to make stiff dough. It should be moist but not too sticky. Roll out on floured surface or waxed paper until 3/8" thick. Cut into rounds with glass and re-roll scraps. Heat on lightly oiled lid until lightly browned, then turn over and cook other side. They need to cook slowly.

Note: These are almost like a fried biscuit, with oats added. I think the quick oats work the best. They have a very unique taste and can be eaten with honey, jam, butter, or just plain warm off the griddle. They also make a unique dinner bread. Add more sugar and they become a sweet bread. Enjoy!

Dinner Rolls

10" or larger Dutch oven; 4 round or square cake pans;
24 briquettes: 8 bottom, 16 top (more if using a larger oven),
Makes 32 rolls

Good:

1 Tbsp. yeast
1/4 cup warm water
3/4 cup warm milk (reconstituted powdered milk)
1/4 cup sugar
1 tsp. salt
1/4 cup oil
3 - 4 cups fine whole wheat flour

Directions:

Dissolve yeast in warm water. Stir in milk, sugar, salt, egg (if using it), oil or shortening and 2 cups of the flour. Beat until smooth, mix in remaining flour. Turn dough onto lightly floured surface; knead until smooth and elastic, 5 -10 minutes. Grease medium size bowl, place dough in bowl then turn dough over so greased side is up. Cover with towel and let rise in warm (not hot) place until double in size, 1 1/2 – 2 hours. Dough is ready if finger impression remains. Punch down dough and form into your favorite type of rolls. For our example you will make pan rolls.

Grease pans that will fit into your Dutch oven. If baking directly in your Dutch oven use foil to line it, then grease foil. The only downfall to this method is you can't pre-heat the oven. I use 9" round cake pans or 8" square pans. This recipe will make 4 pans of rolls, 8 - 9 rolls in each pan. Divide dough into 4 equal parts. For round pans, form 8 balls of dough out of each divided part of dough. If using square pans, form 9 balls of dough for each pan. Place balls of dough equal distance apart in greased pans. Cover and rise 20 – 30 minutes. To pre-heat ovens, place coals on Dutch ovens 10 minutes before baking rolls. Place one pan in each oven, being sure to use foil rings underneath pans. You may have to cook several batches of rolls, or you can stack ovens to conserve charcoal. Bake 15 minutes, then lift lid to check rolls. They should be golden brown when done. Bake longer if necessary. If you were cooking in a kitchen oven you would be baking at 400 degrees.

Better:

Add 1 reconstituted powdered egg.

Best:

Replace oil with butter or butter flavored shortening.
Replace whole wheat flour with white flour.

Cinnamon Rolls

10" or larger Dutch oven; 8" or 9" square/round pans; 24 briquettes: 8 on bottom, 16 on top; Cook 20 min.; Makes 12

Good:

> Use recipe for Whole Wheat Bread
> 1-2 Tbsp. oil (double if using Dinner Roll dough)
> 2 Tbsp. sugar (double if using Dinner Roll dough)
> 1 tsp. cinnamon (double if using Dinner Roll dough)

Directions:

Roll dough out on floured surface into a rectangle 1/4" to 1/2 " thick. (If using Dinner Roll recipe, divide dough in half first). Spread oil or butter over dough; mix sugar and cinnamon together, then sprinkle over dough. Gently roll up dough, starting with the long side until rolled up, ending with seam of roll down. Cut into rounds, 3/4" to 1" thick, depending on how thick you like them. Place rounds in greased pans.

I use 8" square or 9" round pans. Let rise until double 1/2 to 1 hour. Pre-heat Dutch oven(s), then bake on foil ring about 20 minutes or until golden.

Better:

> Use Dinner Roll recipe or any cinnamon roll recipe you have used before.

Best:

> Use white flour.
> Use butter or butter flavored shortening in place of oil after dough is rolled out.
> Sprinkle on raisins or walnuts before rolling.

Note: If you have powdered sugar, make a glaze or frosting by mixing 1 cup sugar with a little water or milk and 1/4 tsp. vanilla to get the consistency you want. Pour glaze over rolls while warm or frost when cool. If using an 8" square pan you must use a 12" or larger Dutch oven. If using 2 ovens, stack cook the cinnamon rolls.

Banana Bread

12" or larger Dutch oven
24 briquettes: 8 on bottom, 16 on top
Cook 1 hour

Good:

1 cup sugar
2 cups whole wheat flour
1/2 tsp. baking soda
1 tsp. cinnamon
1/2 tsp. salt
1 cup dried bananas, broken into very small
pieces, soaked until tender, and drained
1/2 cup oil
1/4 cup reconstituted powdered milk (use
water from bananas when mixing milk)
1 tsp. vanilla

Directions:

Lightly grease 8"x4" bread pan. Mix dry ingredients (first 5) together. After draining water from bananas, mash them with a fork or potato masher.

Cream bananas with remaining ingredients, then add wet ingredients to dry. Mix well. Pour batter into greased pan. Bake on foil ring for 1 hour. Do not add more briquettes. Check after 45 min. Bread is done when it has pulled slightly away from sides.

Better:

Replace whole wheat flour with white flour.

Best:

Replace oil with butter or butter flavored
shortening.
Replace 1/2 of sugar with brown sugar.

Note: You might say, "Banana Bread out of dried bananas?" Yes, this works really well. It is better the next day too, since the banana flavor has had time to permeate the whole loaf.

Corn Fritters

10" lid or larger
15-20 briquettes

Good:

*2 cups corn (dried and soaked and cooked,
fresh cooked or canned)*
1 cup flour
1/2 tsp. baking powder
1 1/2 Tbsp. cornstarch
3/4 cup water
Oil for frying

Directions:

Drain corn and set aside. Mix together dry ingredients. Add water and corn. Pour a little oil onto the lid. When it's hot, drop several spoonfuls of batter onto lid. Fritter batter should be about 1/2" thick. Fry 1 to 2 minutes or until golden. Turn over and finish frying. Remove to plate and continue cooking spoonfuls until all batter is used. You will need to add more oil as you cook all of the fritters.

Better:

Use white flour in place of whole wheat.

Best:

Serve with butter.

Note: These fritters are not deep fried. This is so you can conserve your oil. Just flatten the batter when you spoon it on the lid to cook. Of course, if you have plenty of oil, they can be deep fried, just be careful. These are really good for any meal. Be sure you put a box of corn starch in your storage.

Index

About the Authors

Archie and Linda Dixon live in central California, where they raised 9 children. They were foster parents for 17 years, caring for over 130 children. They have always loved cooking and camping, so when they got their first Dutch oven they knew it would be a life-long hobby. They are active members of The Church of Jesus Christ of Latter-Day Saints and have always felt having extra food stored for emergencies was very important.

Early in 2009 Archie looked at Linda and declared, "We need to write a book about cooking your food storage in a Dutch oven and how to store charcoal. How are all the people who have dried and canned food stored going to cook it when there is no gas or electricity?" That was the beginning of an adventure; one filled with recipes and tasting foods, hot weather and crashed computers. Finally with help from their friends the Medeiros' and the Papins, "Don't be afraid of your food storage…just Dutch it!" was created.